One Square Mile

One Square Mile

The History of Roosevelt, NY
from an Autobiographical Perspective

Sheldon Parrish

To order additional copies of this book, contact:
Xlibris Corporation
1-888-795-4274
www.Xlibris.com
Orders@Xlibris.com
65383

Contents

I start all work by putting God first:

The Lord is My Light and My Salvation
Whom Shall I Fear
The Lord is the Strength of My Life
Of Whom Shall I be Afraid.
Psalms 27:1

It is my story but May God take all the Glory!

A thousand shall fall by thy side, and ten thousand
At thy right hand, but it shall not come nigh thee.
Psalms 91:7

DEDICATION

To My son Sir Damon Parrish:

Son, quiet as it is kept I was the one responsible for your name. I met a cousin back in the1960's who was a radical black thinker during those times and he told me that in order to make sure that his son would always be respected by "all men" he named him "Mister". After telling another cousin the story he also named his son "Mister". Well son, by the time you rolled around the "Mister" thing had become redundant and so I searched for something just as powerful. Evidence of this was that day we were in Wal-Mart in Rock Hill, South Carolina and you had gone further ahead in the aisle and I called your name and the three men also in the aisle turned around only to see I was talking to you. You may or may not understand why, but reactions speak a thousand words.

I am writing this dedication just shortly after watching you graduate from high school. I have mixed feelings today, not because I don't love you because I shall forever, but because of that the negativity which has been forced upon our relationship. I only hope that the missed hours as man and boy are more cherished as "Mano Y Mano." I look forward to an unmanipulated relationship with you. I am proud of the path that originally curved and then you straightened it. This football season put us in the record books as the only father and son tandem to ever make All-County in football at Roosevelt and possibly the county.

AIC, which some people didn't realize stood for, American International College, until I told them, will be all the better because of your well rounded personality and the intelligence you bring on an off the field. Good Luck, my son.

Since 1973 Parrish's have either been players, cheerleaders or coaches and this year, as far we know, will mark the end of an era when Tasheem Granger steps on the field for his last football game. We have enjoyed the opportunity to be a part of something so big!

Acknowledgements

FIRSTLY, I GIVE all Honor and Glory to God. Secondly, I acknowledge my family for their never ending support. Beyond that there are so many people who have given some advice, interviewed and gave information, as well as made pictures and info available about love ones and associates for which I am truly thankful.

I would like to give separate recognition to a group of individuals who were there and supported this project from the onset. Mr. Walter Mackey Jr., Deacon Aaron Scott, Mr. James Hodges. Mr. Samuel Cason, Ms. Diane Robinson and Mrs. J. Sinton. I would also like to acknowledge Rev. Richard Warren, Mr. George A. Jones and Mr. George W Jones for their support and for making space available at the American Legion Post#1957 for interviews. I would like to also mention the time Mr. Gary Battle spent chronolizing events in video and Mr. Dowtin and Mr. & Mrs. Gilbert Evans for there support early on.

Moreover, I would like to thank some people who helped me regain my health from illness that had challenged me during this project. These people gave me a plan for life in which to work with. Truly acting as vessels for God were Dr. Jeffrey Caruso, primary care physician and to Dr. J. Zisfein, Dr. Undavia and all the other doctors and support staff over at South Shore Heart Association of Rockville Centre, NY as well as the staff at the South Nassau Community Hospital.

Before I became serious about my diagnosis of heart disease there were some staff members who were real supportive over at Roosevelt High School. Mrs. Eloise Lloyd, Mrs. Mae Hines, Mrs. Annette Hall and the Culinary staff, "Charmaine", Mrs. Brown, as well as my friends, Mrs. Hamasham, Mrs. H. Carr and Mr. Don Crummell.

I have also been able to plug into my Coach, Dr. Robert Tucker as well as my "comrade in arms" Raymond Mattry on a daily basis (written before he transitioned) and I appreciate the many hours of support. I would be remiss if I did not acknowledge friends and motivators attorney LM Brown and Ms. M. Sanders.

I am also saddened by the fact that my friend Mr. Walter Mackey Jr. transitioned before the completion of this project as well as Mother Dennis, long time member and Minister of music at Calvary Baptist Church and to my colleague and friend Ms. Regina Breland. May God continually grant them "sweet rest".

And God please bless all those names mentioned hitherto and convert their efforts into seeds that you will bless to grow and may anyone that I may have overlooked be covered as well. In Jesus Name Amen.

Parrish Collection

About the Author

SHELDON PARRISH MOVED to Roosevelt with his parents Joe and Ernestine and two brothers, Terence and Todd in August of 1968 from Flushing, Queens NY. His father had come to watch a Roosevelt Varsity Football game with a friend back during the team's undefeated reign (Roosevelt undefeated three years, one year untied, unscored upon (1966-68). His father had a vision of one day watching his sons have a great impact on this town called Roosevelt (Mostly athletic). He wasn't far off in his vision as his sons have tried their best to have an effect on every level, first as players, then coaches and mentors.

The vision started with a move to a house right across the street from Roosevelt Park now known as Rev. Arthur L. Mackey Sr. Park. The family had been to see a house over on Denton, right outside the High school gate. They were all glad that house was not the final choice. The guys now realize that would have meant cleaning up after the daily "after school" fights that have gone on for years. The Parrish's came closer to living on Sherman Avenue but their father and his mother envisioned the three boys' growth completely sucking up the floor plan. Then, there it was, sitting on top of a hill overlooking the park.

The acquisition of this home on Elmwood Ave. started the beginning of a long relationship between this family and Roosevelt.

The oldest son, Sheldon first attended Centennial Avenue School (formerly Quentin Roosevelt), located on West Centennial (West of Nassau Road) the last year of the forced Busing plan. The following year Sheldon attended Theodore Roosevelt (now Ulysses Byas).

Junior High School brought about some memorable experiences in education such as Split-sessions, a teacher's strike and a riot. Split-sessions meant that the High School started at 7:10 am and finished their day by 1pm while the Junior High started at 11:30 am and ended at 4:30 pm. School was closed for a couple weeks due to a teacher's strike that got interesting because of the "scabs" that crossed the picket lines. He also specifically remembered being in Mrs. Levenbrown's Social Studies class in Room 206 when the door busted open and he was told he'd better get up out of his seat and join the enormously huge group already assembled in the hallway. The teacher had forbidden the students from leaving the room that day on the threat of calling a parent. That day Sheldon decided that his parents couldn't have beaten him as bad as this group, and still love him so he decided he would take his chances at home.

Always to large to play PBC/PAL, he began playing football at Roosevelt High in the 9th grade and that was the beginning of a great high school career culminating in a Captainship, Championship and College Scholarship. He played Varsity Football at Division I Colgate University where he was the only freshman to make the traveling team and after majoring in Economics with a Minor in Education, he returned to Roosevelt.

He originally planned on working on Wall Street, but when he found out that, unlike most of his white colleagues, he would have to start his Management Trainee Program in the mailroom, he looked for another direction. The cost of a Long Island Railroad ticket made that level of salary unbearable.

The principal at that time, Dr. Phillip Smith told him that his home school district needed him and he invited Sheldon to come back. Work experiences, summers and social experiences as well as being an active town person has led to a wealth of knowledge about a town off Exit 21 of the Southern State Parkway. Sheldon might be one of a few people that can boast personal experiences with Eddie Murphy, Julius Erving, Chuck D as well as Steve White and Gabriel Cassius. All megastars in their own right.

The author hopes that his version of the history respectfully separates itself from other accounts due to the autobiographical nature of its contents.

Introduction

THIS PROJECT WAS not the original reason for my trip to the Roosevelt Public Library that summer day in 2006. I was attempting to obtain a very viable piece of history that would contain the pride and the essence of the very town that I grew up in. The completion of my other project about the Roosevelt School District would now be held in abeyance on account of my great disappointment with what had originally been rendered as the history of Roosevelt. While reading it, my emotions boiled as the contents ended in the year 1960 and chronicled very little about African-Americans living in the town. The year 1960 is also synonymous with the "white flight" from town. Not symbolic of the deepest sweat African-Americans bore to make this a town one filled with deep conviction and pride.

When discovering the author's name, Harry D. Daniels, I must admit that I was moved to lead a petition to have his name taken off our school building but then I thought of how Ms. Charthern, Principal of the school, had turned the school into a beacon of ethnocentricity; and I figured wherever ole' Harry D. is, he is having quite an unsettling experience. It would be a small issue to call his views "pro white".

Some individuals tried to persuade me to get huge bits of information out of pieces already published. There is some data online, there are some projects written by authors who never lived within the town and most of their information is at least, second-hand. At some point, I will reflect on published quotes because I would like to give honor where honor is due, but it is more my intent to interview as many people as possible to get an actual account as well as reflect on my autobiographical experience which started in 1968. It would appear to me that one who has lived in and among would be a better source then one who never lived but studied about. "Whew"!

The historical overview by Harry D. Daniels dated December 4, 1960 says that Roosevelt's 1,006 acres was known to early Hempstead settlers as the "Great South Woods". Its natural advantages and geographical position (LIE to the Sea) drew house seekers even early on. This town is and has been an important stopping point between Hempstead, Merrick and Babylon. "Trade flowed along this road between shore points and the marketing capital of that time" as Harry. D. Daniels so eloquently states.

I am afraid though that in the end it will be this benefit that will victimize Roosevelt at the hands of gentrification. If I may quote my colleague and fellow classmate Seretta McKnight, "In the 'sixties' the white landowners forgot one thing that has haunted them repeatedly, Never give up the land".

It appears that African-Americans were not present during the first 300 years or so of this town's history. In a piece called African-Americans of Western Long Island by Jerry Komia Domatob he states "As with all Long Island communities it is difficult to establish the exact date when the first African-Americans settled in Roosevelt. As a new spirit permeated the area, land developers took advantage of the location and built houses which they advertised in the African-American Newspapers after KKK activity died down." While speaking with three distinguished gentleman who date back to the "thirties" Jim Hodges, Walter Mackey Jr. and Samuel Cason, it was revealed that during those times we (People of Color) still had to be off Nassau Road by nightfall or risk personal injury or death. Yes, Roosevelt was a "Sundown Town".

One thing we are sure of though is that shortly after 1960, after the marches on Nassau Road and civil unrest Roosevelt became a predominantly African-American town.

In the Beginning

IN 1643 THE Great South Woods was of course, a wooded area which also included a few farms. "The land was being possessed by an Indian tribe called the Merricks. Some colonists from England, (in one account, they are said to be from a town called Hemel-Hemstead another account says Hartsfordshire;) came here by way of Stamford, Connecticut where they lived until religious intolerance and boundary disputes forced their decision to cross the Long Island Sound", says Marquita James Nassau Community College, Professor. Reverend Robert Fordham and John Cramer were said to have been the leaders of this group of settlers. After landing the settlers used different techniques to wrestle the land from the Indians. They even enacted a law that read "By general vote it is so ordered that no person or persons inhabiting within the town or liberties there of, shall plow or break up any planting land for the Indians, nor shall in any way assist them therein under the penalty, forfeiting for every day or part of a days work".

The Indians, faced with wars and local laws of discrimination soon began to disappear. By the early part of the 1800's the town was all-white and was mainly a rest stop for people traveling from Hempstead to Freeport/Merrick. Hempstead was the economic center. Goods from all around were bought and sold in Hempstead. Spirits and liquors flowed freely.

Rum Point, (what Roosevelt was called then) featured farms which produced corn, tobacco, pork and beets in the early years but the evidence of Sweet Clover Diary lends to cattle being raised at some point. Most of the produce items were exchanged for dry goods, furniture and other necessities. The town was then Headquarters for a Rum Smuggling Ring. At a point after the American Revolution there was a general store, three taverns and twelve houses in the area.

Due to change in public sentiment, "The Temperance Movement" brought about a name change. Rum Point, after 1830 was referred to as Greenwich Point. There was a one-room schoolhouse on Washington Avenue where sixty students attended during summer and ninety during winter. As Greenwich Point, (Roosevelt) was primarily a farmland community with the raising of pigs as a major interest. Royal Mollineaux and John Remmert according to Joye Brown, owned the only two stores in the area and they supplied the needs of all the residents. Harry D. Daniels reported that a three room school house was built during this time and also millers came to town. The Mollineaux Brook which was in the post office area was home to the paper mills until the 1900's. There was some smuggling going on through this inlet as well. If you can picture this, my interviewees have told me of a time when the water that flows through Roosevelt Park, once traveled west as far as the Roosevelt Pool area.

There were some legal businesses of course, as Mr. Mollineaux himself owned a large mail order business, selling artificial flies for fishing. The success of the business brought about the need for a post office. The town name had to be changed again due to the fact that there was already a Greenwich Point in upstate New York. By law no post office name can be duplicated.

Theodore Roosevelt had been spending a lot time in the area around the beginning of the century, so they thought to honor him. Some trivia to mention here is that during this time Brookside Avenue was known as Swamp Road, Uniondale Avenue was known as Turtle Hook Road North and Nassau Road was known as South Oyster Bay Turnpike.

It appears that this growth spurred more growth and as the town population began to increase, so did the need to increase school services. Washington Avenue School was built in 1909 but was destroyed by fire. In 1915 Rose Ave was constructed. This school was an elementary and middle school finishing at 8th grade. Most chose Freeport or Hempstead for secondary or high school. In Marquita James' piece she states that Mrs. Denton Roosevelt resident since 1905, recalls that one Black family lived in Roosevelt in a wooded-area in the Southeast end of the village. As the children matured they built houses surrounding their parents home. Since most of the history before this point does not include any African-Americans, it is the 20th century that I choose to dwell.

Chief Kahlid Zahran of the Roosevelt Volunteer Department says that the Fire District was organized in 1912. It is through his interview that I found out that the town of Roosevelt actually ends near Camp Coleman not far from Seaman Court on the East side of Babylon Turnpike. Walter Mackey Jr. had alluded to that during our interview but it became clearer during this interview. Presently, on the West side of Babylon Turnpike, the boundary is near Forest Avenue and Taylor Avenue on Nassau Rd.

approxiamately a quarter of a mile from Camp Coleman. It seems that some time ago Roosevelt was a much larger village as the boundary was once near Seaman Avenue in Freeport. Residents wanting Municipal Water and Sewage and other services provided by the incorporated village of Freeport petitioned to have their section annexed by Freeport in the early 1900's. I had been told since I was little that Roosevelt was "one square mile" when it is really 1.8 square miles. But even with this revelation I will still refer to Roosevelt as "one square mile".

I am also told that Lincoln Avenue used to host races or drill competition between other Hose Companies. Lincoln Avenue once had an arch and spectator gallery like the one behind Greenfield Cemetery in Hempstead. Chief Zahran says that the firehouse on Park Avenue once had barn doors because the original hose company was drawn by horses. This company is known as Hose and Engine#1. The house on Babylon Turnpike is Hose and Engine #3. On Centennial is Alpha Hook and Latter#1. A truck company is housed there as well as Emergency Unit (Ambulatory services and a Fire Police Unit). The obvious question then is what happened to Hose and Engine #2. At times when I've cashed a check at the checking cashing place in Freeport I have made a right turn off Main St. (Nassau Rd.) and traveled down Leonard. At the first stop sign is a fire house. This house used to be the Russell Hose and Engine #2 of Roosevelt. I am told that at one point the town of Roosevelt stretched from the Amory in Freeport to the Plander's parcel now known as Wal-Mart

The number of fire houses in Roosevelt has recently been a topic of discussion as all have been renovated. The Fire Commissioners sought to have all the services under one roof. The Fire Commissioners had intentions on building on that well known property just north of Charles Cleaners on Nassau Road, but it is alleged the that plan met opposition from the "Planning Commissioner".

I received a lesson about "pumping capabilities". Pumping capabilities affect your ISO, which affects your home insurance. Roosevelt presently enjoys a grade 4 rating. Any other rating would have an affect on the insurance rates at each property. Roosevelt has an adequate number of fire hydrants and is well hydranated at 4,000 gallons per minute. It takes the four "Class A" pumpers located one in each house to complete these services. It is obvious that the Chief used this opportunity to explain to detractors why such a small area needs such resources.

There have been sacrifices made by many individuals in Roosevelt. Many of these sacrifices have not been documented. My life has been greatly affected by the sacrifices made after 1968 but I do believe that there were some very key ones made before then. So I sought out those who could take me back as far as possible.

Samuel Cason came to Roosevelt in 1930. He was 10 years old. Mr. Cason is a quiet man but well in his recollection. With the help of a colleague of mine, and niece of his, Diane Robinson we were able to get a pretty good idea of what life was like when he arrived in Roosevelt. One of the more surprising points is that in 2009 it seems people of any ethnicity are comfortable walking Nassau Road at any time, but in 1930, blacks needed to be off Nassau Road by dark.

Life was a lot different in the 1930's. He remembers that the Jackson family was the only one close enough to whites to be on Nassau Road after dark. He says "that about 10-15 black families lived in town when he arrived. The Southside was mostly Portuguese. Mr. Cason said "Jews lived from Mansfield Avenue to about Clinton Avenue or so". I remembered when we moved to town, before the Roosevelt Youth Center was built, the complex was a Synagogue and Yeshiva.

"The roads were dirt until around the sixties", says Mr. Cason The property where Naomi Temple is now located was originally home of the KKK. Between1945-60 the Klan died out in Roosevelt and by the end of World War II Roosevelt had become a village of 8,000 people.

A second gentleman I interviewed, Walter Mackey Jr. stated that "Freeport received its name because it was one of only a few places where goods could be brought in without paying a tariff or tax. Thus, Free-port." His reflections include a group of kids walking a lot of places together because they had no bus fare. He said, "WE would often walk to Roslyn, another hamlet for some African-American families that worked as domestics on the big estates on the north shore of Long Island." When I thought about what kind of walk that would be it seemed virtually impossible until you picture the landscape as almost a straight path with few buildings or obstructions. He remembers that they had to be extremely careful as they went through Garden City. Some things JUST DON'T CHANGE. I asked the question, "Were there any lynchings?" "No," was the response, "but the whites would jump on the blacks and beat then severely. The answer was to return and beat them just as badly." This retaliatory method seemed to reduce the occurrence of these incidents. It was also stated that most blacks maintained a good shotgun or two. Hey Howard Stern. Now who started the beatings?

Roughly around 1946 Mr. Mackey remembered horse farms where kids would go for horse rides. He says Roosevelt High School was a farm at that time and that the Southern State Parkway was only two lanes. Whites remained on the other side of Nassau Road well into the eighties even though they had fled from most of the other parts town. I picked at Aaron Scott, Walter Mackey Jr. and James Hodges until they would tell me the names of some people who may have hindered progress for Blacks as well as those who may have been of great assistance. I identify with one name because I lived in the house that he once owned on Nassau Road, for a short time. In their opinion, "Dr. Bonheim. and his sons tried to help blacks. Sigman of the Sigman Lumber Company was known to deal favorably with blacks. Although no one could remember his first name Mr. Walter Mackey suggested a Lawyer named Rusacow and a gentleman named Russell Smith had influence in helping Franklin National Bank and Roosevelt Savings and Loan to extend credit. Russell Smith sold the first house to an African-American on the North side (Across Washington Avenue) in 1967 for $17,000 at 216 East Clinton to the only African-American plumber in town, Deacon Joe Robinson, father of Diane Robinson. Charles Mereday who owned a trucking company did very well and was able to parlay business with the Town of Hempstead. Walter Mackey Sr. was also able to deal with the whites. Successful businessmen also included the names Baldwin and McKnight.

On the other hand, there was an individual in town who was not very happy with blacks. His name was Rudy Schlegel. He was very powerful in the education process, as well as with rules that controlled the behavior of blacks in Roosevelt. But even though he felt the way he did, he was quite upset about the fact that Hempstead was making claim to John Mackey, Walter's brother. Walter says that early on everyone knew of brother John's talent and when he finished 8th grade he transferred to Hempstead High School. Even though he lived in Roosevelt, Hempstead claimed him as one of there own, much to the chagrin of Mr. Schlegel and others.

After that situation Roosevelt Jr. Sr. High School was built in 1962 with the first graduating class in 1964. Mr. Mackey suggested that the timing was connected to his brother, Hall of Famer, ex-Baltimore Colt John Mackey's emergence as a star player.

Walter Mackey also felt that one of the things that had a great effect on the way blacks lived then was the changing of the zoning laws. In the "forties" most residents had chickens and pigs, Diane Robinson had ducks and turkeys. Dogs didn't need leashes and the parents always knew what yard the kids were playing in by where the dogs were. Animals traveled with the kids. The new laws made it so you couldn't really grow your own food. You had to buy it. Lost was the idea of "Seedtime and Harvest" says Walter Mackey Jr. "Because of these zoning laws you have more people hungry now than back then. We would get on the Long Island Railroad and go out east to the potato farms and get back on the train with a full sack". In some of his last profound words Walter Mackey Jr. said, "We lost a sense of closeness and family because in the old days most times your neighbors bailed you out of trouble. Different organizations were formed to raise money because credit was hard to come by. People fixed meals for each other, ate together, and went places together and always had family prayer together".

An historical prospectus coming from the desk of longtime Roosevelt resident, Aaron Scott states that, "Since 1945 there has been a series of ups and downs economically and educationally in Roosevelt. In the last forty or so, years the village of Roosevelt seems to be in decline. Roosevelt was a vibrant community in the 1940's, mostly Irish, Italian, and Jewish with a few African-American, West Indian and Portuguese from the Cape Verde Islands. Some Portuguese, including "Pop Silver" as we called him were deported some years later".

"Many people of color had their own businesses, namely Charles Mereday (trucking), Lenny Wright (Gulf gas station-Babylon Turnpike and Forest Avenue) and the Bretos, Threadgills and Jacksons (construction) and Mr. Paterson's deli. Some other family names during the "forties" were the Mays, Sintons, Casons, Watkins, Johnsons, Dukes, Fells, and Websters to name a few". Mr. Scott goes further to say "My dad Aaron Scott Sr. was one of the first African-Americans employed by Grumman Aircraft Company during the early forties".

"Roosevelt had six denominations of churches at that time. There was no high school or middle school only elementary schools and a junior high at Washington Rose. The business district was like the business district of Malverne, Merrick or Baldwin today including a movie theatre a restaurant and an A&P supermarket. There was a bowling alley and a diner in the village as well. Later the Sweet Clover Dairy came to Roosevelt. Blue stone roads encompassed the village and with the exception of Nassau Road, there were neither traffic lights nor street signs."

"In the early days there was no gas or oil heat. Coal or wood were the heat sources and later bottled gas. There were no credit cards as the store merchant just trusted you until you paid him. Bread, milk and newspapers were all home delivered. I remember riding horses in the cornfields where the Cerebral Palsy Center is now located, skating and swimming at Washington Lake and at "The Hole" at the east end of Elizabeth and Prospect streets. These were the gathering places during winter and summer. Ducks, deer, turkey, pheasant and small game were hunted in this area during the early forties. Finally, Roosevelt was a real desirable place to live during those early years".

"As a people, we have always had to deal with the hindrances that were often life-threatening" says Deacon Scott. "It appears that the KKK was publicly making their effort around the early 1920's and were said to have had a big meeting in Freeport in 1922. The Klan attitude was subjected to Jews as well as blacks. The organization grew secretly around Nassau County, which in some way, may have helped to foster the ideology behind Nassau being one of the most segregated counties in the country today. Roosevelt's chapter was founded in a house owned by a Mr. Gerring of 59 Babylon Turnpike where Naomi Temple AME Zion (no correlation between the church and the old owner.) presently stands. The KKK activities were nothing like in the South but their presence kept some people from moving here. Jews were moving in at a greater rate at this time and so the harassment of hooded parades and cross burning did have some affect. Probably the most notable cross burning was July 4 1928 but local sentiment had already changed by 1945 and the Klan became a dead issue.

I came across an added bonus the day I went to speak with Alfred Covington. He shared that he had only been a resident since of 1971, so he had a friend of his call me. A woman named Jackie Sinton whose family was in the list Aaron Scott gave. Although Jackie now lives in Jamestown NY and actively works with a group called "The Underground Railroad" she is the only person I know to actually be born in Roosevelt. Dr. Richards from Hempstead a general practitioner did a house call in 1939 and she was born on Bennett Avenue.

She remembers that all the children went to, what she called "the original Black Church", Calvary Baptist. She remembers Elsie Dennis being the organist since she was 4 or 5 years old and my friend Jeffrey's mother still made her way to the organ until this past summer of 2008. Calvary has had a big effect on the early history of the black people of Roosevelt and Jackie spoke of being in a Tom Thumb Wedding where she married a Gordon Wright. In real life, she is the sister-in-law of one of the first African-American educator in Roosevelt, Mr. Charles McIlwain.

She remembers when the lake ran from Roosevelt Park straight through to Freeport with a pond at the end of Frederick Avenue which they swam in as children and like Walter Mackey Jr., she remembers the horse farms where the children rode horses. Ms. Sinton remembers the formation of the Utopia Civic Association, the first organization of its kind and that the Meredays, Mackeys and Jacksons were the big families in town. The community raised pigs and chickens for the "Esquire Club". They in turn would raise money at parties given on Prospect. Even until this day it is not uncommon to see a block party on the Southside of Roosevelt ie: Tim Key on Decatur and the Underhill group. I was lucky to receive a very special packet in the mail from Mrs. Sinton which includes some documents and pictures from of her time spent in Roosevelt.

In the Black Americans Series of Western Long Island by Dr. Jerry Komia Domatab, he says "as a new spirit permeated the area, land developers took advantage of the location and built houses which they advertised in African-American newspapers after KKK activity died down. The African-American population grew and by the 1950's it reportedly covered six square blocks. Washington Ave marked the dividing line between whites and blacks, with whites dominating the North side and blacks residing on the South flank. The all 'Negro' area south of Washington Ave was called 'The Section". But as time moved on, Blacks came seeking better, less congested neighborhoods where they could live the American dream of nice house, clean yard and suburban schools. However as soon as they moved in, the whites would relocate elsewhere. Thus segregation occurred in Roosevelt either through voluntary departure or natural osmosis" (The writer was kind, as many whites snuck out under the cover of darkness). He further says that by 1963, the Theodore Roosevelt school was 98 percent non-white and by contrast Centennial was 98 percent white. As a result, the Board of the State Education Department was compelled to order the desegregation of Roosevelt Schools. After fighting the "good fight" the plan went into affect in the mid-sixties. "The Princeton Plan" called for moving students from their neighborhoods in order to balance out the white and non-white ratio. This busing plan is said to be the main factor for white exodus." In 1965 after going to court over the busing issue, a man by the name Robert Spillane was installed as the new Superintendent. He was appointed to implement the plan and then enforce it. Despite heated opposition the schools were desegregated. Although some whites had left the eastern and northern parts of Roosevelt hitherto, some still had intended on staying on the West side.

When I came to Roosevelt in the summer of 68, it was the beginning of the last school year for busing. I was bused from my house over by Roosevelt Park to Centennial. How I remember the names Ms. Unyss, Cliff and Gene three of the more popular bus drivers. The following year I walked to Theodore Roosevelt for 6th grade.

The author goes on to say, "In their determination to join the massive exodus of 'white flight', many white residents became the first 'slumlords' of Roosevelt. In the midst of internal accusations, frustrations, disgust and fears more than half of the middle class of blacks left Roosevelt and moved to other parts of Long Island. The placed welfare families' affected the school system by an impact of 26.6% of its population. A large number of these educationally disadvantaged students required remedial and other special programs. The burden of tax increases fell on the Black middle-class because the white middle-class had left and the welfare recipients paid no income tax".

Realtors began to use illegal techniques called "Block busting" where scare tactics were used to convince property owners that their homes' value would plummet. Moreover, the security issues would be an increasing problem due to the minority influx, inducing owners to sell at real low prices. Middle-class blacks began meeting with whites and they banded together. The situation became more intensified when an article appeared in the New York Times, "Harlem Comes To Long Island, Negroes Invade Roosevelt" alleging that Nassau County Department of Welfare was going to turn Roosevelt into a "Welfare dumping ground" in order to deal with the increasing amount of vacant houses. Some homeowners just walked away before they could find a suitable buyer. They had hoped that HUD would come up with a program that would still maintain a racially balanced working class town. That never happened. Even into the new millennium Roosevelt is still plagued by a tax burden as well as the Socio-economic effects on the village and the school district.

Nevertheless after all the dust cleared, the people who stayed in Roosevelt made it a town where battles for equality were fought and won, decisions were made and implemented, time was invested and well spent to make this town a very viable town. A town where the people were proud to walk the

SHELDON PARRISH

parade route on holiday as kids wore uniforms with the team sponsor on back. Those trips to Carvel sometimes win or loss, but the reward for the homerun or a touchdown was that big "double cone" that earned you the respect of your team mates.

In the following sections there will be a lot of names mentioned. The risk with a task of this magnitude is that an oversight might occur and names unintentionally omitted. I apologize before hand for such oversights and however small the contribution this town is appreciative for your efforts. God Bless!!!!

"Organizations Pave the Way"

PBC/PAL

GEORGE JONES WAS able to afford some time to give us a perspective on the development of one of the most influential organizations in Roosevelt. Influential because if you grew up in Roosevelt you were in some way impacted by the PBC in the early days and it's switch over to PAL. Actually before the PAL, the organization was a group of smaller organizations switch started around 1963. PBC ran a boxing program (Fred Swint), a traveling basketball team (Jim Simpson, Univester Smith and Frank Brown) a track team (Tina Holmes), A drill team (Lola Curry) and the Sharpshooters bowling league (Christina Evans). The Roosevelt Junior Sports Club (Richard Warren) ran the town baseball program on three divisional levels; juniors, minors and majors. I would like to mention Mr.Robert Powell Sr., Mr.Oscar Glass,Mr. Gilbert Evans, Mr.Elmer Bryant, Mr.George Blackburn, Mr.Walter Dennis and Mr.Al Crummell football teams played a schedule that is unheard of now but on Saturday they played in a PBC league and on Sunday they played in a league called L.I.M.F.O.L. Mr. Alleyne was the Patrolman in-charge. There became a time when the Coaches Association split and when PAL came to town the other organizations could not compete with PAL's financial resources.

During the school year (besides a variety of athletic and mentoring programs) the day program consists of a child's pick up from home in the morning, being transported to the PAL for breakfast then on to each child's school. In the afternoon, pickup from school, homework-study sessions and activity skills back at the PAL, dinner and then the trip home for a very affordable cost. Recently the Program Director became Todd Parrish a longtime PAL employee and supporter of their programs. He will continue to make PAL an efficient and viable entity.

Equal Opportunity Council (EOC)

To look into the vision of the EOC you must first go through John Kearse, long term Chief Administrator. Mr. Kearse also transitioned to the next life in 2007 but left a resounding legacy. First being born in Brooklyn, raised with ten siblings, moving on to Delaware State University and achieving a Masters from Fordham University, Mr. Kearse embarked upon a life time of work for the Minority community. "Well educated and well trained in the realities of African-American communities, Mr. Kearse was one of the few street organizers of the 1960's who was able to become a institution builder in the 1970's and then champion of a major agency in the 1980's. Step by step he helped remove the system's injustices that had hurt all poor and powerless people on Long Island and devastated the lives of hundreds of thousands of dark-skinned Americans, locking them into cycles of poverty and hopelessness.

Among African-Americans on Long Island, Mr. Kearse has been virtually unique as an individual who is both willing and able to make a stand against the abuse of African-Americans and Hispanics communities. For that commitment and ability he has wielded enormous economic, political and social power, building the Equal Opportunity Commission (EOC) of Nassau County Inc. into an unparalleled power. Most unique, that power has originated from the support of the people.

It was August of 1970 when Mr. Kearse assumed the reigns of CEO after a very maligned and heated racially motivated struggle. "Mr. Kearse's first action as head of the EOC was to organize a 3,000 person bus convoy to Washington, DC in support of the continuation of the National Full-Year Head Start Program. The program had been doomed to close because the legislation that created the program contained a sunset clause requiring renewal every two years. Mr. Kearse managed to obtain an interview with Donald Rumsfeld, who was the Director of the Federal Office of Equal Opportunity, at that time. Mr. Kearse persuaded Mr. Rumsfeld to support continuation of the Head Start program. The 3,000 people left Washington with Mr. Rumsfeld's promise in hand. Head Start's place in the national consciousness was secured and has remained to this day.

The EOC has offered a lot of different programs to the economically challenged in the village of Roosevelt. Some programs have been geared towards the job development piece where the EOC prepares individuals for the interview process as well as the actual seeking of employment. There are also programs designed to help our youth to be productive human beings. With the increase of our Latin community the EOC has had to meet the new challenges of this population which have experienced some culture and language barriers. Nevertheless, I expect that the new Director Iris Johnson will carry the torch to build on the legacy of her predecessor.

Roosevelt Library

The Roosevelt Public Library began in 1934 in a one room donated space at One Whitehouse Avenue with donated books, funds and volunteer staff made up of community members. Within four years (1938), the Library had outgrown its temporary quarters and relocated to a new slightly larger temporary facility at 60 Washington Avenue. Between 1938 and 1994, the Library continued to expand and the demand for services increased such that it became necessary for the Library to relocate from Washington Avenue to Rose and Mansfield Avenues to mobile trailers and finally to its current location today on Nassau Road and West Fulton Avenue.

While temporary Library services existed in Roosevelt prior to 1994, Roosevelt Public Library facility was characterized as the smallest structure and in the worst condition of any of the fifty-four (54) public libraries in Nassau County. Prior to construction of the 1994 permanent structure, the Roosevelt Library building consisted of a one-room converted garage with a "dug out" basement where the physical limitations of the building allowed only for a maximum of nineteen (19) seats at reading tables. The building was filled and every available closet, corner and wall crammed to capacity. The Director's Office (11 feet by 11 feet) was shared by a part-time secretary, a supply cabinet, a periodical collection of 6,000 magazines, a file cabinet and two desks. Limitations were so severe that the temporary structure had to be supplemented by two leased mobile trailers, one used as a Children's Room and the second used as a storage area for the Library's noted special Black Heritage Collection

In 1994 a two-floor ADA accessible building was built at which time the Library became a true community center serving the 15,000 resident, Roosevelt, as well as residents of other Nassau County neighborhoods. In 1998 the Library opened the Lower Level of the new facility, providing additional services to the community such as a computer center and adult education.

Today, the Roosevelt population exceeds 16,000 and in step with libraries across the country. The Roosevelt Public Library has reevaluated how to meet the growing needs of their growing and changing community. Thus, in addition to its main function of providing free access to written and technological information, the Library evolved to become the central neutral facility to host cultural programs, special Children's programs, and lectures. The Library has also become an Adult Education center for computer health, legal and medical topics.

Technological advances as well as increasing social awareness and cultural programs have put a tremendous demand on space in the current building. The community relies heavily upon the facility not only as a resource center, but as a center for the study of human arts, providing education, culture, and developmental mental activities. The Library is a neutral space where all members of the community are welcomed.

Auxiliary Police

I had the pleasure of speaking with co-founder Mr. Murray who says that he started the Roosevelt unit with his partner Willie Manicks and some friends Gilbert Evans, Al Vaughn and Jim Hodges in 1975 after first becoming a member in the Lakeview unit. In the early days Mr. Murray reports that expenses were funded by the group. They paid $3.00 dues and any extra cost was paid out of pocket.

Somebody came up with an old station wagon that they put the emblem on the doors and gas, insurance etc. came out of the expense money. They were very appreciative of the people at McZeno service station formerly on Nassau Road as they were the only station to extend them credit.

Originally a Lt. Hobbs was the overseer but then a long tenure was forged with Inspector Blankethorn. The Auxiliary officers went through 13 weeks of training and then received second hand uniforms from Police headquarters in Mineola. They were the police officers eyes and ears and being a family oriented group, Mr. Murray was always concerned about harm to his officers so at the first sign of law breaking activity the police were radioed.

The Auxiliary officers watched people get off buses and sometimes followed the women to their door to make sure they arrived safely. They did not make themselves real obvious but often times a flick of the light once inside let the officers know that their vigilance was appreciated. They were also out on Halloween and Teen Canteens and Centennial basketball games, but they were never allowed to serve after midnight. Mr. Murray also reports that they had a good working relationship with the Police Department.

Mr. Murray retired and turned the reigns over to Mr. Robert Olden in 2001. He says the unit gets free gas, cars and insurance these days.

Mr. Murray came to Hempstead as a baby in 1934 and moved to Roosevelt in 1966. He is enjoying life after retirement from his day job in construction. The 3rd generation of his family shares his love and he says the reason why he has stayed in Roosevelt is because of the people. Sadly, he feels that the handwriting is on the wall that 20 years from now few African-Americans will live in town.

Roosevelt Chamber of Commerce

The Roosevelt Chamber of Commerce was organized December 1983 and operates as a "Not-For-Profit" corporation registered in New York State. Its purpose is to advance the commercial, industrial, civic, educational and general interests of the Unincorporated Village of Roosevelt and its environs. As a membership based organization we are obligated to provide our members with the kind of leadership they require in the effort to accomplish our purpose. As an association of business men and women we are committed to the success of all of the Roosevelt community's local businesses. To achieve this, the Chamber acts as a focal point for many different activities which affect the business and the community environment of Roosevelt. From time to time we will provide business training seminars covering topics such as Working Capital, Management, Insurance and Bonding, Marketing and Advertisement, and how to do business with Local Government. If there are any other topics that you might be interested in please let us know.

We act as lobbyist for various business district needs; such as better police protection, more aggressive rubbish removal. The Chamber will also act as a communication resource center and network by bringing those decision makers and business influencers to membership meeting to help local merchants get their views heard to better understand our changing times and community.

We would be more than happy to have you as a member whether you have a business or not. Thank You and hope to see you soon,

Roosevelt Chamber of Commerce Board Members Mr. Allan W. Thompson Interim-President Ms. Yvonne Simmons vice-President/ Treasurer, Ms. Catherine B. New, Recording Secretary, Ms. Clara Eromosele, Mr. Leo Fields, Mr. Stuart Nisbett, Mr. Douglas Mayers, Mr. Richard Warren

Alumni Association shall exist to promote the welfare of the Roosevelt school district and community by: Contact Us (www.rooseveltalumni.net/aboutus)

Since 2002 Roosevelt Alumni Association, Inc. has existed to promote the involvement of alumni in the progress of the Roosevelt school district and community. By providing a a forum so that Roosevelt alumni may establish and continue relationships, stimulate positive interaction between the school district and community, we provide leadership as the means for Roosevelt students to achieve educational excellence.

Mission Statement

The Roosevelt Alumni Association shall exist to promote the welfare of the Roosevelt school district and community by:

- Providing a forum so that Roosevelt alumni may establish new relationships and continue existing ones
- Encouraging the alumnus/alumna to assume involvement in the progress of Roosevelt school district and community
- Stimulating and fostering an environment of positive interaction between the Roosevelt school district, Roosevelt Alumni Association and the Roosevelt community at large.
- Organizing, sponsoring and promoting events that will strengthen the existing cultural and social background of the Roosevelt alumni, students, and community.
- Provide leadership and the means for Roosevelt students to achieve educational excellence

Keshia Richmond

As former president and co-founder, Ms. Richmond is dedicated to achieving the mission of the; Her leadership and vision continues to help propel the association to new heights responsible for leading strategic planning, leading fundraising activities, and developing the organizational agenda from the associations inception

Ms. Richmond grew up in the beautiful Appalachian mountains of southwest Virginia among a family of coal miners; She moved to Roosevelt at the age of eight and graduated from Roosevelt High School in 1991; She went on to earn her Bachelor's of Science degree from New York Institute of Technology in Business Administration: Management of Information Systems.

Ms. Richmond has held various high profile IT (Information Technology) positions at companies such as General Electric, The Federal Reserve Bank of New York and Computer Associates. She now operates, Richmond Technology Solutions, Inc., an award winning Internet consulting firm based in Deer Park, NY

Robert Dixon—President and co-founder

Rob is known for his dedication and hard work. He works closely with the Board members to achieve his vision for alumni. Rob was instrumental in our first annual Alumni Day. He championed the support of alumni from as far away as Maryland and coordinated our efforts with Project Grad

Robert J. Dixon is a veteran of Roosevelt, having grown up there while attending its schools beginning in pre-K until he graduated in 1989. In 1994, he graduated from New York Institute of Technology with a Bachelor's of Science degree in Engineering and Technology.

Mr. Dixon is accomplished in the field of engineering and has contributed his expertise at distinguished companies such as Northrop Grumman, Periphonics (Nortel), and Interdigital Communications, Inc. Mr. Dixon is currently employed with Motorola Inc. (Enterprise Mobility Division), a successful mobile computing manufacturer based in Holtsville, NY, where he specializes in wireless technologies.

Robert truly believes that Roosevelt's people (alumni, parents, students and faculty) can deliver substantial growth for the students, as long as unity & teamwork prevails.

Jennifer Scott—as co-founder and Treasurer, manages the finances and administers all fiscal matters. She devises the annual budget and ensures the development and board review of financial policies and procedures.

Ms. Scott is a 1989 graduate of Roosevelt High School who has resided in Roosevelt her entire life. Ms. Scott holds a Bachelor's of Science in Electrical Engineering from SUNY New Paltz and serves her industry as an AutoCAD

Drafter.; Ms. Scott is currently Employed by Northrop Grumman as an Engineer

When asked why she decided to join the association, she replied, "I wanted to create a way where alumni of Roosevelt can come together. With there being so many successful alumni, the children of the community really need to see that successful people have graduated from Roosevelt. Provide leadership and the means for Roosevelt students to achieve.

D.A.D.S. for Education

"Dads Are Doing Something"

(Submitted by Raymond Mattry one week before his passing)

DADS FOR EDUCATION is an organization/program of men (fathers, grandfathers, uncles, cousins, brothers and any other men). The focus is to have men be involved in the process of educating children through volunteering in individual schools in an effort to fulfill the mission of the school district.

The mission is to volunteer and support students, parents, staff, and the community by enhancing the learning environment through the active presence of men in individuals schools.

Although it is a rough task to get some males to be role models, research shows that the male role model is a critical and essential ingredient in the learning process.

Raymond Mattry was the man behind the local chapter of DADS, which is a national organization until his passing in the Spring of 2009. Raymond and I grew up some few blocks away from each other but actually stood on two different sides of the road philosophically most of our early years. It wasn't until we decided to do a "Holiday Basket" campaign for the less fortunate that we began to see our "later in life commonalities". One thing we both believed that through all the inconsistencies by adults in the community the only real victims were the kids.

Because of life experiences he was more concerned with a child's safety to and from school, the gang issue, and making sure the process afforded all kids the right to be equal with their counterparts in other towns and school districts. He was controversial because of his in your face; call a lie a lie approach. Because of my size I could not have the same approach because I found that when entering a room my size already created a certain climate.

My energy was always focused on the student/athlete and giving kids positive things to do especially when adults don't realize that the financial cutbacks over the years is really what caused the troubled streets. This, because the kids had very little positive programs offered. I also thought the coach/player relationship was a great way to mentor and sometimes nurture a kid who had no other choice but to see you in that light.

The last couple weeks in Raymond's life we became extremely close with a common bond of relationship with God and the need to take care of ourselves health wise. I had gone away for a few days during this time and neglected to call him and he told me off because he said, "I have become accustomed to you listening to my breathing over the phone and telling me when I sounded strong or not and when I had fluid present".

The evening before he transitioned we had engaged in conversation about event insurance that was supposed to I guess; create a new world order for us or something. His ministry is missed by many who depended on him to get on their case about not being the best they can be. I pray God's peaceful transition for my brother Raymond Mattry.

Julius Erving

BESIDES THE FACT that there were rumors around town that there was this basketball player who could jump high enough to snatch quarters off the top of the backboard at the Theodore Roosevelt Elementary School gym, I also had the opportunity to grow up watching a future Hall of Famer. I have probably mentioned at some point that Saturdays were active in that we woke up in time for the usual cartoons and then mom had our weekly chores planned for us. We had to have these chores done before we left the house. Me and my friends also had to have our game or two in before the bigger boys came and kicked us off. Julius was never one of the guys to kick us off but he would come onto the court not long after and tie up his landing gear (sneakers). My experiences became more personal my last year or so of school. I am not sure of the order of events but I can say that when I made the Junior Varsity Basketball team, I was given a pair of gold and a pair of blue suede reconditioned sneakers said to have been donated by Julius the year before. The Varsity had new ones.

A more direct experience happened the summer of my junior year. I was walking up the hill towards the gate of Roosevelt Park when I noticed a brown-paneled Ford station wagon pull into the park. I observed that the occupants were Dr. J and his former teammate Al Skinner (NY Nets). They were headed to the tennis courts. My best friend Steve Smith was walking with me and although he could not play a lick of tennis, he remembered someone in his house had an "ole Brownie" (Brown wooden tennis racket) so he ran all the way home to retrieve it just so he could play. When Steve returned, we challenged them to doubles. Al didn't play the greatest at that time either so he and Steve kind of got in the way. I challenged the "good doctor" to a singles match. I was one of Ms. Emily Moore's protégé's and although it wasn't basketball, I beat Dr. J in a set 6-4.

During my senior year, my football scholarship was being threatened by a failed school budget vote and an Austerity budget. As the captain of the football team, I was chosen by the Athletic Department to represent the school in an effort to raise funds to support the sports program. The first step, Dr. J came to the gym and a few of us students took pictures standing behind him sitting on a stool, in his Nets uniform, holding an old ABA basketball acting like he was checking it's pulse with a stethoscope.

These pictures became huge posters that went into all the train stations in NYC sponsored by Converse. I believe George Holt got the opportunity to play against "Doc" in a one on one. Then there was a big media event at Penn Station in Manhattan where a fellow student Corliss Bailey '76 and I did "photo ops" with Julius Erving. Thirdly, the Nets donated partial proceeds from one of their games at the Nassau Coliseum. Sports went on as usual and I earned my scholarship to Colgate University. Thank you, Julius Erving. The following is the normal account of what you find on Julius's professional career in query.

(Newsday)

Position	*Small forward*
Nickname	Dr. J
Height	6 ft 7 in (2.01 m)
Weight	210 lb (95 kg)
Nationality	*USA*
Born	*February 22, 1950* (1950-02-22)
	*http://en.wikipedia.org/wiki/Image:Flag_of_New_York. svg*Roosevelt, New York
High school	Roosevelt High School
College	*University of Massachusetts*
Draft	12ᵗʰ overall, *1972*
	Milwaukee Bucks
Pro career	1971-1987
Former teams	*Virginia Squires 1971-73,*
	New York Nets 1973-76,
	Philadelphia 76ers 1976-87
Awards	

- ABA MVP (1974, 1976)
- ABA First Team All-Star (1973-76)
- ABA championship with New York Nets (1974, 1976)
- Led the ABA in scoring (1973, 31.9 ppg) and in 1974 (27.4 ppg)

- Five-time ABA All-Star (1972-76)
- Holds ABA career record for highest scoring average (28.7 ppg) in a minimum of 250 games
- NBA MVP (1981)
- *Sporting News* NBA MVP (1981)
- All-NBA First Team (1978, 1980-83)
- All-NBA Second Team (1977, 1984)
- 11 NBA All-Star Games (1977-87)
- Two-time NBA All-Star Game MVP (1977-after scoring 30 points, 1983-after scoring 25 points)
- One of only five players in pro basketball history to score more than 30,000 career points
- Upon enshrinement, ranked in combined ABA/NBA history top 10 in the following categories:
    - third in scoring (30,026, 24.2 ppg),
    - eighth in games played (1,243),
    - seventh in minutes played (45,227),
    - third in field goals made (11,818),
    - fifth in field goals attempted (23,370),
    - third in most free throws made (6,256) and first in steals
- Jersey retired by both the Nets and the 76ers
- NBA 35th Anniversary All-Time Team (1980)
- NBA 50th Anniversary All-Time Team (1996)
- *J. Walter Kennedy Citizenship Award* (1983)
- Jackie Robinson Award presented by Ebony Magazine (1983)
- American Express Man of the Year (1985)

Hall of Fame 1993

Eddie Murphy

When I was a senior at Roosevelt High School Eddie was a sophomore. Back in the seventies we had a unit in school called the Hall patrol. This group, made up of mostly football players stood posts in the center of the hallway to make sure that traffic flowed and that it traveled on the right side of the hallway. Most mornings this young guy would come past my post on his way to his class. He would somehow wind up in a comedy routine after beginning with "How ya doing big fella" and it seems like every morning a different mini skit would take place at my expense. Laughingly, all I could say was "Man get to class". After graduation I didn't see Eddie for a few years. I was away at school and he was here doing his thing. The story has it that during Eddie's senior year in high school another Roosevelt alum Derek Lawrence would let Ed borrow his car so that he could go to the Comedy clubs on the North Shore of Long Island. Eddie's real beginning. When I returned home from college I went through a very severe club dancing phase. I wound up at most of the places that played "club" or "house music" from Hempstead to Manhattan.

A guy by the name of Charles Belcher used to give parties in Hempstead at a place called the Native New Yorker every Wednesday night. This party was called the "Wednesday Night Wiggle". There I was, in my uniform, parachute pants, cut-up t-shirt," going for what I know" (dancing hard) on the dance floor when I hear a voice from behind me saying "Get down Crusher, Yeah . . . .) It was Eddie being amazed by my movement. I could get down for a big "fella". He would frequent this party during the SNL days up until shortly after 48hrs.

One night I was visiting Roosevelt alum, Ronald Murphy, when he asked what I was doing later on that evening. The next thing I knew I was driving across the 59th street bridge headed to NBC studios in Manhattan. I parked and we went upstairs. When the elevator opened there was a line. We waited, but somehow Clint another close friend of Eddie's and Roosevelt alum (he was in the opening jail scene with Eddie in 48 hrs. as Eddie's cell mate) peeked his head out of a side door and he saw us. As he called to us we heard all these sighs from people in the line. (haters) We walked down this real tight hallway backstage and in the first dressing room we passed were the "world renown" Smothers Brothers. We walked through to the main auditorium. Not long after, part of the cast came out for the warm up they do before "Live" starts. During the warm-ups the Smothers Brothers and

Eddie get into this conversation that winds up being a staged argument. They jump him and the next thing I know Eddie is calling my nickname, "Crusher" out loud. He was yelling my name, and I froze. I wish I knew that one was coming. Maybe I could have responded in a way that could have started my acting career. Well who knows . . . . ?

Shortly, thereafter I went to see 48 hrs. at the Sunrise Multiplex in Valley Stream. I was enjoying the movie when right at the part when the character Gantz (played by Richard Defoe) pointed a gun in Eddie's head; The Movie stopped!!!!!! There was a brief pause and then Eddie stood up in the back of the theater and yells, "Yo, What the F—is going on in here? The place went nuts and then the movie resumed. By the time the movie ended "Big Money" was gone.

The next time I saw Eddie was the last time in person. It was at the Paradise Garage, a very well known underground club on King Street in Manhattan, (much respect to DJ Emeritus Larry Levan). I wish I could take the time to explain the culture of this club but another time, and as usual Larry was pounding the club when I noticed an entourage go through the club. When I went to the fruit and juice lounge I realized it was Ed or "Big Money" as the insiders called him but with all the attention all I could do was shake his hand and trade a smile and a nod. I did catch the act, of another Roosevelt alum there one night, "show person" as well as R&B/Gospel performer Carolyn Harding.

During the mid-eighties I lived at Dr. Bonheim's old house on Nassau Rd and one Friday while relaxing after a hard week of work. Derek Lawrence, then Vice-president of Eddie Murphy Productions, stopped by the house. A small group of us usually assembled there on weekends. When he came in, he asked if we wanted to hang out. Now normally (because of my home training) I passed on invitations that don't include the destination, but this time my gut told me it was cool. We got dressed quickly, got in our cars and followed Derek (unknowingly) to the Nassau Coliseum. When we got there we parked. Derek went in front and we followed. He spoke to one of the employees who directed him to another employee. We followed. The next employee walked with us and the next thing I knew we were sitting in the 8th row of a Prince "Purple Rain Concert". Prince was throwing sweat all over us. It was great!!! We went to an after party at a place called Spit, in of all places, Levittown. When we got there Madonna was performing. It was the early days when she had the two black dancers behind her. (Holiday) What a NIGHT!!!! The following is a Newsday account of the professional life of Eddie Murphy. I have provided these accounts so that although my personal experience best serves me and historical account needs to serve others as well.

Biography (Internet-Newsday)

Eddie Murphy's road to international stardom started innocently enough in Roosevelt, Long Island, where his parents moved to from Brooklyn when he was ten. Roosevelt, a compact one-square mile of middle-classdom, boasts an unusually disproportionate alumni of internationally renowned celebrities such as shock jock-cum-actor Howard Stern, NBA Hall of Famer Julius "Dr. J" Erving, rap supergroup Public Enemy's Chuck D and Flavor Flav and vocalists Aaron and Damian Hall. Not bad for a postage stamp town.

Eddie Murphy absorbed the lifestyle of Roosevelt like the proverbial sponge, focusing on his youth experiences to draw the basis of "The Barbecue" and "Drinking Fathers." Both skits are side-splitting accounts of an afternoon family get-together, with near-disastrous results. But it takes a great storyteller with nerves of steel to display so openly one's life to a live audience, to have them laugh at the situation, but more importantly, laugh with you. Eddie Murphy's live comedy act reveals quirks, bends and touches of irony.

Closets are thrown open, allowing skeletons to rattle as loud as they can. A perfect example is the classic "Ice Cream Man," a virtual time machine for any listener trained in childhood to hear the ice cream truck above all other sounds and react like Pavlov's dog. On the flip side of the piece, Murphy reveals the joint cruelty/pleasure children can sometimes elicit.

Eddie Murphy was at the right place at the right time for America. He recalls his frustration, early on, in getting the powers that be to recognize his unique abilities: "I started out in comedy when I was 15. I used to do bars and gong shows, stuff like that. I used to call agents all the time and say, 'I'm a funny guy! Can you give me some work?' And they'd say, 'Get outta here!'" The question begs to be answered: Where are those agents now? Probably still kicking themselves over their colossal inability to recognize talent. Broadway Danny Rose they ain't!

Murphy went on to become the talk of the burgeoning New York comedy circuit and eventually parlayed that into a 1980 audition for "Saturday Night Live." His four-year stint with the show produced such memorable characters as the pimp Velvet Jones, the intense and angry poet Tyrone

Green, Mr. Robinson, a parody of Mr. Rogers, and his most memorable character, Gumby.

Greatest Comedy Hits brings together material culled from various phases of Murphy's stand-up career, as well as snippets from several of his timeless movies. From his landmark and controversial "Eddie Murphy Raw" in-concert movie, directed by a then-unknown Robert Townsend, Murphy involves his audience in "The Barbecue," "Drinking Fathers," "Singers," "Cumin' Hard" and "Skeleton In Closet," while one of Murphy's most memorable "Saturday Night Live" characters, "'Buckwheat'" and the nonsensical "Hit By A Car" are culled from his debut album.

An aside: Murphy performed "Hit By A Car" in his first-ever appearance on "The Tonight Show," and immediately received the venerable Johnny Carson's stamp of approval. Murphy's brilliant and uncanny impressionist skills are accented on "Old Jew" from his 1988 film "Coming To America," and "Grandma Klump," from his zany 1996 "The Nutty Professor," which, incidentally, received a 1997 Oscar for Best Makeup, certainly a payback for the long hours Murphy spent under heavy makeover.

The essential Eddie Murphy is both irreverent and endearing. There are no sacred cows in his world. Take, for example, "Singers," on which such vocal icons as James Brown, Luther Vandross, Michael Jackson and Stevie Wonder receive his sting. You just know Eddie Murphy had to be blessed with a strong voice himself, which he intersperses within his skits for emphasis and flavor, never failing to get a rise from his audience. That success gave Murphy the confidence to cut two best-selling singles; his 1982 "Boogie In Your Butt" from Eddie Murphy, and a collaboration with Rick James on the gold 1985 release "Party All The Time" (which actually sold a million copies, but was released before the RIAA changed gold status from 1,000,000 to 500,000 and gave one million the platinum ranking it now holds).

You gotta love Eddie Murphy because the man took us through the bullishly Reaganesque 1980's with a bravado, yet charming comedic style that revitalized a seemingly interminable industry slump. Don't bother looking; there is no more successful black actor on the planet. Actually, having generated over $2 billion in revenue from "48 Hrs.," "Trading Places," "Beverly Hills Cop I, II & III," "The Golden Child," "Another 48 Hrs.," "Coming To America," "Boomerang," "The Distinguished Gentleman," "Vampire In Brooklyn," "The Nutty Professor" and "Metro", it is safe to say that Murphy's ranking as a leading-man is immeasurable.

Chuck D

I knew Chuck to run around as a young boy but I remember him more as a young man. Probably the most important issue to define our relationship early on was my ignorance of the music business. At the time I believed that Rap/Hip Hop would be a fly by night genre' needing no real creditability. I take this opportunity to admit my ignorance publicly. I think at the time my feelings had a lot to do with my affection for club/house music. Although Chuck was a little younger than me, we had occasion to hold conversation usually on the "activist level". I remember when he, Hank and Keith Shockley and this brother named Ujima first worked at WRYC, a radio station in the basement of the Roosevelt Youth Center on Mansfield Ave. Then the guys launched their mobile disk jockey tour where they did local gigs including Roosevelt High dances. My partner Don Crummell and I had what we billed as a "Disco Extravaganza" at the VFW Hall in Uniondale. We had Spectrum perform and we just barely broke even. As we competed against a popular concert event at the Nassau Coliseum and also another affair, but most of all, I had been told by my mother to "change the date" because it was Good Friday (Christian mother). I guess mom knew best.

Soon after the group became Public Enemy and all the success since then has been well documented. During the 80's the DJ of the group Terminator X launched an independent project called "Valley of the Jeep Beeps". On the project was a cut called "I Hate School" by the "Juvenile Delinquents". I was asked by the production team if I could make it possible to tape a video at Roosevelt High School. I had a great relationship with the School Superintendent, Rodgers Lewis and the Business Manager, Mr. Springhorn.

On face value, I think they approved up until a couple days before shooting the video. Public Enemy had a shooting, the day before our shooting. An announcement was made so that people could be there to be used as extras. The homeowners on Lincoln Ave. and many people in the surrounding blocks were quite unhappy. On-lookers had trampled yards and destroyed property.

I had to promise that the same scenario would not happen to the school. I relayed the message to all who had to know ahead of time and everyone else was on a need to know basis. I was responsible for getting the extras needed for roles in the video I got my brother Terence and a friend of the family to play the roles of 2 security guards needed. There were a few scenes where kids were needed and since I was working for the Roosevelt Unit of the PAL that summer I used some of the kids from one of the camp groups. I was even able to include myself as one of the bodyguards at the end of the video as the group ran out of the building and into the patented Terminator Van. All were satisfied with how it worked out and there were about ten people present who did not belong. A plaque once hung in the principal's office symbolizing this effort. My experience is rather with Public Enemy rather Chuck per se so I have included his personal accomplishments as per Wikepedia:

Biography

Carlton Ridenhour was born in *Roosevelt, Long Island*.[1] After graduating from *Roosevelt Junior-Senior High School*, he went to *Adelphi University* in *Long Island*, graduating with a *bachelor of arts* degree in *Graphic Design*.

Upon hearing Ridenhour's demo track "Public Enemy Number One", fledgling producer/mogul *Rick Rubin* insisted on signing him to his *Def Jam* label.[2]

Chronologically, their major label albums were: *Yo! Bum Rush the Show* 1987, *It Takes a Nation of Millions to Hold Us Back* 1988, *Fear of a Black Planet* 1990, *Apocalypse 91 . . . The Enemy Strikes Black* 1991, *Greatest Misses* 1992, and *Muse Sick-N-Hour Mess Age* 1994. They also released a full length album soundtrack for the film *He Got Game* in 1998. Ridenhour also contributed (as Chuck D) to several episodes of the *PBS documentary* series *The Blues*. He has appeared as a feature artist on many other songs and albums, having collaborated with artists such as *Janet Jackson, Kool Moe Dee, The Dope Poet Society, Run-DMC, Ice Cube* and many others. In 1990, he appeared on "*Kool Thing*", a song by the *alternative rock* band *Sonic Youth*. In 1993, he executive produced Got 'Em Running Scared, an album by *Ichiban Records* group "Chief Groovy Loo and the Chosen Tribe".[3]

In 1996, Ridenhour released *Autobiography Of Mistachuck* on *Mercury Records*. In November 1998, he *settled out of court* with Christopher "*The Notorious B.I.G*" Wallace's estate over the latter's *sampling* of his voice in the song "Ten Crack Commandments". The specific sampling is Ridenhour counting off the numbers one to nine on the track "Shut Em Down".[4]

In September 1999, he launched a multi-format "supersite" on the web site Rapstation.com. A home for the vast global hip hop community, the site boasts a TV and radio station with original programming, many of hip hop's most prominent DJs, celebrity interviews, free *MP3* downloads (the first was contributed by multi-platinum rapper *Coolio*), downloadable *ringtones* by *ToneThis*, social commentary, current events, and regular features on turning rap careers into a viable living. Since 2000, he has been one of the most vocal supporters of Internet music *file sharing* in the music industry.

He loaned his voice to *Grand Theft Auto: San Andreas* as DJ Forth Right MC for the radio station *Playback FM*. He appeared with *Henry Rollins* in a cover of *Black Flag*'s "Rise Above" for the album *Rise Above: 24 Black Flag Songs to Benefit the West Memphis Three*. He recently contributed a chapter to Sound Unbound: Sampling Digital Music and Culture (The MIT Press, 2008) edited by Paul D. Miller a.k.a. *DJ Spooky*.

Politics

Ridenhour is extremely politically active; he co-hosted *Unfiltered* on *Air America Radio*, testified before *Congress* in support of *peer-to-peer* MP3 sharing, and was involved in a 2004 rap political convention. He continues to be an *activist*, publisher, lecturer, and producer. Addressing the negative views associated with rap music, he co-wrote the essay book *Fight the Power: Rap, Race, and Reality*, along with *Yusuf Jah* (*ISBN 0-385-31868-5*). He argues that "music and art and culture is escapism, and escapism sometimes is healthy for people to get away from reality", but sometimes the distinction is blurred and that's when "things could lead a young mind in a direction."[5] He also founded the record company Slam Jamz and acted as narrator in Kareem Adouard's short film *Bling: Consequences and Repercussions*, which examines the role of *conflict diamonds* in *bling* fashion.

In an interview with *Le Monde* published 29 January 2008[6], Chuck D stated that rap is devolving so much into a commercial enterprise, that the relationship between the rapper and the record label is that of slave to a master. He believes that nothing has changed for African-Americans since the debut of Public Enemy and, although he thinks that an Obama-Clinton alliance is great, he does not feel that the establishment will allow anything of substance to be accomplished. He also stated that French President Sarkozy is like any other European elite: he has profited through the murder, rape, and pillaging of those less fortunate and he refuses to allow equal opportunity for those men and women from Africa. In this article, he also defended a comment made by Professor Griff in the past that he says was taken out of context by the media. The real statement was a critique of the Israeli government and its treatment of the Palestinian people. Chuck D stated that it is Public Enemy's belief that all human beings are equal.

In an interview with the magazine *N'Digo* published in late June 2008, he spoke of today's mainstream urban music seemingly relishing in the addictive euphoria of materialism and sexism, perhaps being the primary cause of many people harboring resentment towards the genre and its future. However he has expressed hope for its resurrection, saying "It's only going to be dead if it doesn't talk about the messages of life as much as the messages of death and non-movement", citing artists such as *NYOil*, *M.I.A.* and the *The Roots* as socially conscious artists who push the envelope creatively. "A lot of cats are out there doing it, on the Web and all over. They're just not placing their career in the hands of some major corporation."[7]

- on an episode of *Johnny Bravo*.

Film appearances

- He is the narrator of the 2006 documentary "Quilombo Country", directed by Leonard Abrams.
- He is prominently featured in *Hip Hop: Beyond Beats and Rhymes*, a 2006 documentary by Byron Hurt.
- He is prominently featured in the 2008 film *The Black Candle*, directed by *M.K. Asante, Jr.* and narrated by *Maya Angelou*.

Gabriel Cassius

I really didn't know Gabriel all that well, but well enough to have casual conversation around town but mostly at the park. One Sunday I remember Eddie, Derek and Dujuan (Bodyguard) and the crew were at the park hanging around the red Porsche and the black Mercedes Sport (in the 80's) cutting up and having a good time. About forty yards away on a bike rack sat Gabriel. He sat there, his arms folded, with such a look of confidence. I detected his very thoughts so I asked him and he replied, "One day I am going to be that big. I said "Yeah"? How? He said "I can't discus it, but watch". Since then I have seen him star in movies such as New Jersey Drive, Get On The Bus and several others featuring roles acting along side people like Denzel Washington.

I had the biggest surprise in June of '09 when I happened to touch basis with a friend and I noticed that she was friends with Gabriel so I contacted him with the same story I just told and he agreed to give me an interview over the phone. I am so appreciative of the time Gabriel Cassius took to give me a phone interview on June 7, 2009. It was so good to hear a voice I have become accustomed to hearing on the big screen and even most recently on the television show 24. It was a pleasure to flashback to times past, including the bike rack story. He admitted that he did not remember the particular conversation but he knew it was consistent with both his mindset and what other people have said to him about that juncture of his life. When I told the bike rack story hitherto, I believed for years that his path for success went through Eddie Murphy because he was at Roosevelt Park that day. In reflection, Gabe says "that it was more like seeing Eddie as an inspiration that day and he probably blurted out some things as a result of meditation on his goals."

I found out in this conversation that they did not actually crossed paths until much later on. But like Eddie, Steve White and many others, Gabe spent a lot of time in the 300 wing hallway watching the ladies and "snappin" (cracking jokes) and being late to class or eventually cutting that class because you were to late. Gabe says that "thoughts of Roosevelt bring on a certain irony in retrospect because what he learned when he did go to class helped to sustain him during his career. The education available at Roosevelt High School then seemed to be superior to what I encountered from my peers who had attended public schools in other areas of the country including New York City schools". Even though he moved from Brooklyn to Roosevelt in 1976 and left in 1983, he is quite proud that he has done well to secure his future with only a Roosevelt High School diploma in his educational background. But, he also states that staying in Roosevelt after graduation had become stifling to his creativity and he relocated to a studio apartment in Harlem where he had the opportunity to network with fellow thespians. The move helped to foster and further formulate his mindset as an "artist" and gave him a base for cultural exposure and greater sources to expand his creativity.

Gabe, like most struggling actors, actresses and models etc. waited tables and hustled to survive while attending a private acting class. "Up on 96th st. there was an old-time, theater actor by the name of Nathan George who was a friend of a friend, that gave these small classes. Nathan had been in the movies, "One Flew Over The Cuckoos Nest", "Klute" and "Brubaker" (I must mention Barbara Streisand and Robert Redford here).

One of the reasons why he and Eddie did not cross paths early is because Gabe was not hanging out in the comedy clubs trying to make it. He sought to be "classically trained as a serious dramatic actor." It does appear that Gabe and Steve White do have similar roots because the Director Spike Lee is responsible for both gentlemen's first acting roles in major motion pictures. Gabe answered an "Open Call" for the movie "New Jersey Drive". "Spike liked what I did in the room that day so he gave me the lead part."

Gabe and his management team decided that if he wanted to go to the next level, he needed to move to "Cali". He bought a one-way ticket on the old Tower Airlines in 1995 and he has been there ever since. He has added directorship as another facet to his career gem and he is directing a $40 million dollar project "Takers" starring Paul Walker, Chris Brown and Ti. An action film due out soon.

All with a Roosevelt High school education. It was sad to have to explain to him that things just ain't like they used to be. The band, the shop classes and the planetarium are all pleasant memories now. I obtained the following from IMDB.com

Actor:

- *2000s*
- *1990s*
G-Force (2009) . . . . Carter
"*24*" . . . . Robert Galvez (4 episodes, 2009)

- *Day 7:3:00 a.m.-4:00 a.m.* (2009) TV episode . . . . Robert Galvez
- *Day 7:2:00 a.m.-3:00 a.m.* (2009) TV episode . . . . Robert Galvez
- *Day 7:1:00 a.m.-2:00 a.m.* (2009) TV episode . . . . Robert Galvez
- *Day 7:11:00 p.m.-12:00 a.m.* (2009) TV episode . . . . Robert Galvez

Dough Boys (2009) . . . . Simuel

"*CSI: Crime Scene Investigation*" . . . . *Detective* Williams (2 episodes, 2008)

. . . aka "CSI: Las Vegas" (South Africa: English title: informal alternative title) (USA: syndication title)

. . . aka "C.S.I." (USA: short title)

. . . aka "CSI: Weekends" (USA: promotional title)

. . . aka "Les experts" (Canada: French title)

- *Art Imitates Life* (2008) TV episode . . . . Detective Williams
- *The Happy Place* (2008) TV episode . . . . Detective Williams

"*CSI: Miami*" . . . . Jeff Murdock (1 episode, 2007)

. . . aka "CSI: Weekends" (USA: promotional title)

- *Internal Affairs* (2007) TV episode . . . . Jeff Murdock

"*Justice*" . . . . DA Reyes (1 episode, 2006)

- *Shark Week* (2006) TV episode . . . . DA Reyes

"*Grey's Anatomy*" . . . . Taylor Tressel (1 episode, 2006)

- *Sometimes a Fantasy* (2006) TV episode . . . . Taylor Tressel

Sixty Minute Man (2006) (TV)

Brothers in Arms (2005) . . . . Linc

"*Law & Order: Trial by Jury*" . . . . Kenny Thompson (1 episode, 2005)

- *The Line* (2005) TV episode . . . . Kenny Thompson

Their Eyes Were Watching God (2005) (TV) . . . . Sam Watson

. . . aka Oprah Winfrey Presents Their Eyes Were Watching God (Australia: DVD box title)

"*CSI: NY*" . . . . Jerald Brown (1 episode, 2004)

- *Officer Blue* (2004) TV episode . . . . Jerald Brown

"*Line of Fire*" . . . . Henry Denard (1 episode, 2004)

- *Eminence Front: Part 1* (2004) TV episode . . . . Henry Denard

"*The Handler*" (1 episode, 2003)

- *Big Stones* (2003) TV episode

"*Skin*" . . . . Billy (3 episodes, 2003)

- *Endorsement* (2003) TV episode . . . . Billy

- *Secrets & Lies* (2003) TV episode . . . . Billy
- *Pilot* (2003) TV episode . . . . Billy

"Presidio Med" (1 episode, 2003)
- *Breathless* (2003) TV episode

Black Hawk Down (2001) . . . . Kurth

"The Practice" . . . . Daryl Johnson (1 episode, 2001)
- *Inter Arma Silent Leges* (2001) TV episode . . . . Daryl Johnson

"First Years" . . . . Jean (1 episode)
- *Porn in the U.S.A.* (????) TV episode . . . . Jean

15 Minutes (2001) . . . . Unique
 . . . aka 15 Minuten Ruhm (Germany)

Ritual (2001/I) . . . . J. B.
 . . . aka Tales from the Crypt Presents: Revelation (USA)
 . . . aka Tales from the Crypt Presents: Voodoo (Philippines: English title)

Bedazzled (2000) . . . . Elliot's Cellmate/Angel
 . . . aka Teuflisch (Germany)

Lockdown (2000) . . . . Cashmere

Harlem Aria (1999) . . . . Anton
 . . . aka Destiny—Einmal ganz oben stehen (Germany)

"The Crow: Stairway to Heaven" . . . . Soleil Hazard (1 episode, 1999)
- *Closing Time* (1999) TV episode . . . . Soleil Hazard

Modern Vampires (1998) (TV) . . . . Time Bomb
 . . . aka Revenant (UK: video title)
 . . . aka Vamps (Philippines: English title: theatrical title)

Black Dog (1998) . . . . Sonny
 . . . aka Black Dog (France)

The Wedding (1998) (TV) . . . . Hannibal
 . . . aka Oprah Winfrey Presents: The Wedding

Fallen (1998) . . . . *Art* Hobbes

Buffalo Soldiers (1997) (TV)

Don King: Only in America (1997) (TV) . . . . Jeremiah Shabazz

"New York Undercover" . . . . Mason / . . . (2 episodes, 1994-1997)
 . . . aka "Uptown Undercover"
- *The Unthinkable* (1997) TV episode . . . . Tony
- *School Ties* (1994) TV episode . . . . Mason

Get on the Bus (1996) . . . . Jamal

Lone Star (1996) . . . . Young Otis

Nightjohn (1996) (TV) . . . . Outlaw
"*The Parent 'Hood*" . . . . Bobby (1 episode, 1996)
   -   *An American Class President* (1996) TV episode . . . . Bobby
"*Homicide: Life on the Street*" . . . . Derek Sherman (1 episode, 1996)
   . . . aka "Homicide" (USA: informal short title)
   -   I've Got a Secret (1996) TV episode . . . . Derek Sherman
"*Silk Stalkings*" . . . . Deon Wilkes (1 episode, 1995)
   -   Glory Days (1995) TV episode . . . . Deon Wilkes
"*Law & Order*" . . . . Dewey Lattimer (1 episode, 1995)
   . . . aka "Law & Order Prime" (USA: informal title)
   -   Purple Heart (1995) TV episode . . . . Dewey Lattimer
New Jersey Drive (1995) . . . . Midget

Writer:

Takers (2010) *(post-production)* (written by)

Producer:

Takers (2010) *(post-production)* (executive producer)

Self:

Paul Mooney: Jesus Is Black—So Was Cleopatra—Know Your History (2007)
   (V) . . . . Himself
   . . . aka Paul Mooney: Know Your History—Jesus Was Black . . . So Was
      Cleopatra (USA: DVD box title)
Reflections on Paul Mooney (2007) (V) . . . . Himself
Brothers in Arms: The Making of a Modern Western (2005) (V) . . . . Himself
The Essence of Combat: Making 'Black Hawk Down' (2002) (V) . . . . Himself

Steve White

I searched the internet and could not find the data about Steve that would satisfy my sense of purpose. I ran into his online store and decided to email the "contact us" email address and Steve responded. He called me on the phone and we had a great conversation full of flashbacks etc.

Steve grew up on Eddy Road in Roosevelt the sight of my first paper route. He did not remember making collecting the fee for the newspaper a weekly adventure. I believed something was wrong with him, at first, but I was so wrong. He is very intelligent and very talented which has led to success with Stand-up Comedy as well as major motion pictures.

Steve would often act as if he was losing his mind or emulate a particular cartoon character and it usually made my visit to his steps the longest of all, every time. I think he could have been acting that way because in his early years of education he was a "private school kid" who often wondered why all his friends walked by him on the bus stop every morning, on their way to schools in Roosevelt.

He originally graduated from Grace Lutheran School and then his parents enrolled him in St. Agnes for which he says, "I stayed for a weekend." Around this time he too became a Newsday carrier and wound up doing the same route. In all these years, this conversation brought that to light.

Steve came to Roosevelt schools in the tenth grade and he admits that he was probably funnier there then he was at those private schools. I reminded him that during that era you had to be able to "snap". You almost had to be better at that, then fighting. We didn't fight much then because it wasn't cool unless you had become too embarrassed by someone snappin' on you.

Upon graduation from Roosevelt Steve traveled two paths. One path to Nassau Community College and later on to Adelphi University, the other, Stand-up Comedy. His first gig was at "The White House" in Massapequa, then Governor's, Chuckles and East Side Comedy. After becoming frustrated about not being able to snag a commercial spot, he attended a party at "Big Money", excuse me Eddie Murphy's old house in Bubble Hill, New Jersey.

The problem had been that Steve did not have a Screen Actors Guild (SAG) card save for union membership for actors. Eddie happened to be working on "Coming to America" and told Steve to come to the set that next week and he would take care of him. The role was only a minute or so, but enough to get the Sag card.

Spike Lee happened to come to the premier of the movie and Steve figured he couldn't lose anything by asking for a reading and Spike instructed him to see his casting director Robbie Reed. He auditioned for "Do the Right Thing", and got the part.

One of Spike's major rules was that you had to be on set everyday whether you were working that day or not. He believed in creating a family environment by the cast being together everyday. Steve says, "It was like being in Spike Camp." I asked did he have to pay that Long Island Railroad fee for daily travel but Steve informed me that his 1986' 280zx which he calls the "Quiet Storm," was in affect for those trips.

Martin Lawrence and others were in this family. Since his role did not work everyday, our star managed to learn jobs on the set from "grip" to directing and he figured, at some point he would have use for those skills. When Malcolm X was being filmed Steve paid his own bill and went as an understudy to Spike. That film was shot in South Africa.

Shortly after, Steve returned to "the Velt" and Spike actually came to Roosevelt to help in a fundraiser. The event took place in the gym at Roosevelt High School with coverage by Newsday for purpose of raising funds for a short movie Steve produced called "Love Anyone" with Emily Moore playing a role. These days Steve has a lot on his plate with helping his wife raise a set of twins in LA. After leaving Las Vegas, where he homed his skills in real estate and doing the morning spot for a Hip-Hop station Wild 102 Steve won the San Francisco Comedy Competition which he was "numero uno" out 32 other comedians. His work in the feature film "Skin Deep" yielded him an esteemed American Black Film Festival-Best Actor in a Feature Film Award. The following is a bio from the internet care of IMDB.com

Steve White (born February 13, 1964, in *Brooklyn, New York*) is an *African American actor* and *comedian*, best known for his roles in *Spike Lee* films.

Actor:

"Cuts" . . . . Preston / . . . (2 episodes, 2006)
- *Strictly Biz-Nass 2: Biz Nastier* (2006) TV episode . . . . Preston Gaines
- *Carpal Kids* (2006) TV episode . . . . Preston
Skin Deep (2003) . . . . Michael

Ping! (2000) . . . . Agent Bruce Mechanic

"Martial Law" . . . . Jeff (1 episode, 2000)

-   *Deathfist 5: Major Crimes Unit* (2000) TV episode . . . . Jeff

Goosed (1999) . . . . Lawrence

"The Jamie Foxx Show" . . . . Kyle (2 episodes, 1997)

-   *Do the Write Thing* (1997) TV episode . . . . Kyle
-   *Act Like You Love Me* (1997) TV episode . . . . Kyle

"Arli$$" . . . . Lance Rinker (1 episode, 1997)

-   *Kirby Carlisle, Trouble-Shooter* (1997) TV episode . . . . Lance Rinker

Breakdown (1997/II)

Get on the Bus (1996) . . . . Mike

Bulletproof (1996) . . . . Veteran Cop

"Martin" . . . . Dr. Friendly (1 episode, 1996)

-   *The Tooth Will Set You Free* (1996) TV episode . . . . Dr. Friendly

"The Show" . . . . Reginald Bryant III (1 episode, 1996)

-   *Pilot* (1996) TV episode . . . . Reginald Bryant III

"In the House" . . . . Emcee (1 episode, 1995)

-   *Boyz II Men II Women* (1995) TV episode . . . . Emcee

Clockers (1995) . . . . Darryl Adams

Open Season (1995) (as Steven C. White) . . . . Leon

"Hangin' with Mr. Cooper" . . . . Steve Warner (4 episodes, 1994)

-   *Clothes Make the Man* (1994) TV episode . . . . Steve Warner
-   *True Romance* (1994) TV episode . . . . Steve Warner
-   *Instant Replay* (1994) TV episode . . . . Steve Warner
-   *Between Friends* (1994) TV episode . . . . Steve Warner

Mona Must Die (1994) . . . . Clarence

. . . aka Ein fast perfektes Verhältnis (Germany)

"Living Single" . . . . Elmo Sable (1 episode, 1993)

. . . aka "My Girls"

-   *In the Black Is Beautiful* (1993) TV episode . . . . Elmo Sable

Malcolm X (1992) . . . . Brother Johnson

. . . aka X (USA: poster title)

Other People's Money (1991) . . . . Richard

. . . aka Riqueza ajena (USA: Spanish title: video title)

Mo' Better Blues (1990) . . . . Born Knowledge

"Glory Days" (1 episode, 1990)

-   *Blastin' Away the Blues* (1990) TV episode

The Adventures of Ford Fairlane (1990) . . . . Detective

Harlem Nights (1989) . . . . Patron
Do the Right Thing (1989) . . . . Ahmad
Coming to America (1988) . . . . Subway Guy
   . . . aka Prince in New York (Europe: English title: video title)
. . . *All the Marbles* (1981) . . . . Body Builder
   . . . aka The California Dolls (Australia) (USA: reissue title)

Revenge of the Cheerleaders (1976) . . . . Aloha Basketball Team
   . . . aka H.O.T.S. III (UK: video title)

Producer:

Skin Deep (2003) (*associate* producer)

Writer:

"Tompkins Square" (1 episode, 1996)
  -   *Episode #1.1* (1996) TV episode (writer)

Second Unit Director or Assistant Director:

Malcolm X (1992) (director trainee)
   . . . aka X (USA: poster title)

Production Manager:

She-Devils on Wheels (1968) (assistant production manager)

Thanks:

Heckler (2007) (special thanks)

Self:

- *2000s*
- *1990s*
"Freedom of Speech Comedy Show" . . . . Himself (1 episode, 2008)

- *Episode #1.1* (2008) TV episode . . . . Himself
"Late Friday" . . . . Himself (1 episode, 2001)
- *Episode #1.30* (2001) TV episode . . . . Himself

"The Magic Hour" (1998) TV series . . . . Regular (unknown episodes)
What's Wrong with Sports in America? (1997) (TV) . . . . Himself
"Comics on Delivery" (1997) TV series . . . . Himself (unknown episodes)
     . . . aka "C.O.D." (USA: short title)
"Tompkins Square" . . . . Himself (1 episode, 1996)
- *Episode #1.1* (1996) TV episode . . . . Himself
"Def Comedy Jam" (1992) TV series (unknown episodes)

He has worked with Lee five times (*Do the Right Thing* in *1989*, *Mo' Better Blues* in *1990*, *Malcolm X* in *1992*, *Clockers* in *1995*, and *Get on the Bus* in *1996*). From 1992 to 1997, White performed *stand-up comedy* on *Russell Simmons's Def Comedy Jam* on *HBO* and he also had a recurring role on the *Fox* comedy series *Hangin' With Mr. Cooper*.

Carolyn Harding

Bio

Born in Burderop Park, England to Robert and Della Harding. Carolyn is the oldest girl of four children, Bobby, Kim and Ricky. Her vocal career started in 1977, a student at Roosevelt High School, Roosevelt, Long Island. While busy doing community plays and concerts; Carolyn was discovered by a lady named Lori Butler. Lori became manager and took Carolyn under her wing and helped to develop the studio professionalism that Carolyn still holds strong today. Later, balancing a production deal and the New York school of Theatrical Arts, Carolyn landed a job with Disney World. Her first long term engagement away from home. Under the strict guidance of a very talented team of directors, stage managers, musicians, stylists, dancers and entertainment executives Carolyn developed and grew into a well-polished performer. This is the foundation on which she has based the many levels of show business that her career has been so blessed to have experienced.

Brother Ricky introduced Carolyn to Dance Music in 1986. He was an original member of the famed Paradise Garage. As did many of the key players in dance music at that time, Ricky passed away in 1990. Ricky was my biggest fan. In his memory Carolyn vowed to have a dance record released every year. She has done that and more. Some producers include Winston Jones, Dave Shaw, Joey Negro, Seamus, Deep Zone, Soul Solution, Keri Chandler, FUKUTOMI, and Shinji Takeda, DJ Kawasaki and Akakage among others. Carolyn has recorded for many of the top Dance Labels in the U.S. and abroad. Her records have climbed to the tops of numerous charts across the world. Some of her earlier works include background vocals for Sal Soul Orchestras, Jocelyn Brown, Louis Vega to name a few.

Carolyn has performed in many countries for thousands of adoring fans. When I sing, I wish to touch people in the most positive way. She has shared the stage with such greats as Phyllis Diller, Little Richard, Sheryl Lee Ralph, Shannon, Gwen Guthrie, Sylvester, Thelma Huston, Shirley Bassey, Jeff Krasner, Herb Williams and so many more. Carolyn has had the honor of performing as one of the Shirelles. She has created an enormous following in the dance market worldwide.

After a two ½ year tour up and down the eastern seaboard, in 1993 Harding returned to New York with her three year old daughter Brittney and settled on Long Island where she met and married Jeff Johnson. Looking for a weekly income at her craft, Carolyn was introduced to the wedding industry. As a freelance vocalist Carolyn worked for Hank Lane, Steven Scott, Starlight Orchestras, Ken James, Dance Jock and a host of other companies. Late in 1996 Harding started working with Peter Greco Music & Entertainment as a freelance vocalist. Soon after, Peter made a move to his own north shore office and Carolyn began a new career as Production Consultant, which also included other office management duties. Carolyn dedicated many hours in the years to follow cultivating new skills on the business side of the industry.

In May of 2000 just four months after the birth of her son Jaylin; Carolyn suffered injuries from a car accident. This made it difficult for her to maintain such a heavy schedule at the office and performances with Peter Greco. With much regret Carolyn had to resign from her position and commit more time to rehabilitation and family. By October, eager to participate in a business that she has grown to love, As a freelance artist I saw so many nightmares, where brides were crying because a bandleader didn't even care about special song presentations that had been requested months in advance Carolyn decided to open an office of her own CAROLYN HARDING MUSIC. "I want to be there for as many brides as possible to help in any way that I can". Carolyn quickly establishing a relationship with an elegant, five star Caterer on the south shore, As well as an Events Coordinators. They shared the same ethics and commitment to excellence, quality and professionalism as Carolyn. She takes pride in customizing each package to fit the individual needs of the client. In spite of its newness the business started to grow and grow. Corporate Events, Weddings, Anniversaries, Birthdays, Night Clubs and Track Dates the phones started ringing.

Harding's first love has always been Jazz and Blues. Her repertoire expands decades also including R&B, Pop, Gospel, Island, Jewish, Italian, Irish and other ethnic specialties. 2003 Carolyn was in the studio much of the year collaborating with Jazz impresario Al MacDowell on several production efforts. The first single "What is Love" was release early in 2004 on Gossip Records. Also that year named the ultimate Star Seeker Winner by Norwegian Cruise Line, Carolyn has been sailing the high seas performing for thousands of guests throughout the Caribbean as a headlining act on the main stage.

Currently, Carolyn has recorded her latest musical effort produced and written with her brother BeWise (Bobby), "All Because of You" on Deep Haven Music. BeWise and Carolyn's daughter Brittney are singing background on the tracks and performing live; keeping it all the family. This will be Harding's Neo Soul / R&B debut after making such a strong presence in the Dance Music world for more than two decades.

I first met Carolyn in a Roosevelt High School hallway when some jealous young ladies were about to her harass her. I was on hall patrol at the time and I perceived the situation as a great way to be chivalrous to an attractive female. Even then her star shined In the early years I had opportunity to see Carolyn perform but the proudest time was the night I was in attendance at the Paradise Garage. That was the last place I saw Eddie as well. I wonder if celebrated DJ, Larry Levan realized his true drawing power. (LLRIP)

Eric Jenkins

Eric Jenkins has served as one of my role models. I can never forget the picnics at Eisenhower when we were young. I remember those tall pots boiling the corn and crab. The menu also included clams. I remember those clams being shucked and my first experience with "clams on the half shell". I have eaten many bushels since.

During my college years often times when I would not be motivated to work out and prepare for the upcoming football season, I would see this older gentleman (my neighbor) huffing and puffing as he ran laps around the block with his stick in his hand for any dog confrontations. I guess he was keeping in shape for any potential on-foot apprehensions. My conscious would then bother me and I would change clothes and work out. He was always so serious and professional but sometimes found time to play football on the block with us. Roosevelt's own was recently honored by the following.

honoring
ERIC JENKINS
Detective Lieutenant

Eric Jenkins began his law enforcement career when he joined the Nassau County Police Department on April 16, 1965. After completing recruit training, he was assigned to patrol duties in the Fifth Precinct.

In 1967 he was promoted to Detective and assigned to the Detective Division where he served in the Vice Squad and Community Relations Bureau.

In 1971 Eric was promoted to the rank of Sergeant and assigned as a patrol supervisor in the Fourth Precinct.

Five years later, he was promoted to the rank of Detective Sergeant. As a Detective Sergeant he returned to the Detective Division where he remained until his retirement. He began supervising Detectives in the Seventh Squad and in 1984 he was designated Deputy Commanding Officer of the Fifth Squad.

In 1987 Eric was promoted to Detective Lieutenant and designated Commanding Officer of the Third Squad where he served until 2002, when he was designated as the Commanding Officer of the Special Investigations Squad.

Eric has enjoyed many accomplishments throughout his 41-year career including his distinguished position as Team Leader of the Crisis Negotiation Team.

While dedicating himself to the Nassau County Police Department, Eric also pursued his own education. He earned an Associates Degree, Bachelors Degree and is a graduate of the prestigious FBI National Academy.

In 2001 Eric suffered a stroke that threatened to end his law enforcement career. He underwent extensive speech and physical therapy, determined to overcome the challenges of his illness. In less than 4 months he was able to return to full duty status in the Police Department.

Eric will be enjoying his retirement with his wife of 46 years, Joan, his two children Darryl and Dawn and his granddaughter, Crystal.

Eric's legacy to the NCPD will continue long after his retirement as those he inspired carry out their mission with the same dedication and integrity that he displayed throughout his entire career.

Richard P. Warren

True, Mr. Warren may have lost a half a step with age but you would never tell it by his still busy schedule. Along with his wife at his side he continues to have people scratch heads with the projects he still takes on. As I researched I found that Mr. Warren is a Committee Member of the Jim Simpson Memorial Scholarship Fund, Board Member of the Chamber of Commerce, Coordinator and facilitator for the newly renovated VFW Post#1957, on the pastoral staff at Naomi Temple as well as some private ventures. Now that may not be much to some, but to say that he is a few years on the other side of sixty makes it more impressive. He also is the Coordinator for the Memorial Day Parade and part of the Greek fest planning committee.

To get the true essence of the man though you would go back to the sixties. Mr. or Rev. Warren was a multitasker before it was even popular. He was my brother, Terence's baseball coach on the junior level and I would watch the games at Roosevelt Park. Firstly, he was always good at motivating the pitcher as he would cheer for you on every strike and then talk you right into the next strike. There was one strategy I copied from him (Best form of flattery) when I coached Junior High baseball at the school. Whenever there was a man at third, with less then two outs and the batter walked, I would teach the batter to start running from home and not stop until he reached second base. This always caused some kind of confusion in the field and a lot times, the benefit was a run scored.

While he did this with his evening time he usually ran a business during the day. His main business was Security the perfect extension of a successful and esteemed military career retiring as a Sergeant Major in USAF. He was the first African-American to do some things in the military but he won't often talk about that, but I do know in 1978 he was heralded as being the first African-American local businessman to have a million dollar contract which he signed with then, Con Edison of NY. I learned two things about Mr. Warren then; firstly, he had the ability to make you feel good about yourself. Every time he would see me he would perform in front of small groups of people about. me being the "Crusher" (my nickname) and how I was going to play in the Pro's. I never made it that far but he always made me feel like I would. Secondly, with this contract he tried to hire as many local people from Roosevelt as he could. He even hired me that summer to take floaters from Roosevelt to work in the Con Edison yards in NYC so that they would have jobs. He even supplied the car and the gas. It is a shame that the workers never respected that because their behavior such as drinking on post, missing their trips around the yard (punches) and not showing up for work is what made this situation different from the intent. Mr. Warren will quickly tell you though that the key to his longevity is that he "Never looks back" no matter what the outcome.

Not long after I came home from college Mr. Warren had a Security company which he made me the Vice-president of Operations. Either through my over-eagerness or through employees not maximizing their work time, it didn't work out, but during that time I was taught and then given the opportunity to work on a contractual bid. Then I presented my numbers to bid for the security contract at Roosevelt School District back in the 80's. We got the contract and that whole experience has been revisited for use on a few occasions since then. Many people asked me on occasion, "How could I work for him?" and I would always say he couldn't pay me for what he was teaching me.

The latest chapter in his life is what is most impressive to me. There is a certain shrewdness about a good businessman that some don't understand, and what they don't understand, they don't like. But when I found out that he was a "Man Of God". I felt such joy. I have a personal relationship with God, through his son Jesus. I have not been called to pastor although we are all called to minister. I have come through some things for which I give God all the Glory, but just someone else that I can talk about the goodness of God with, has been a blessing. I needed those kinds of conversations to get me through a workday at Roosevelt High School some days as well.

Emily Moore

In the "About the Author" segment of this project I spoke about a middle school experience that caused me to have to walk out of class without permission from the teacher. I was in Mrs. Levenbrown's class in room 206. She was a good teacher and usually quite inept at maintaining her class but this was a different kind of day. See the murder of Dr. Martin Luther King Jr. had such an effect on mobilizing people until the people who killed him probably wished they hadn't and just harassed him the rest of his life.

It was the early seventies now and the major white flight had taken place. Blacks were the majority race in town and for a lot of people that was a new unfamiliar place. There was a woman from the Freeport /Roosevelt area who had gone to Morgan State University and was party to a lunch counter protest. Then upon graduation, went on to the Peace Corps to help people in underdeveloped countries. She was now on staff at the Roosevelt Junior Senior High School.

During a time when we were in the process of fighting for the simple things, Emily Moore was empowering students to fight the good fight because she felt quite frankly, "No struggle, No Peace". Ms. Moore was fired by the school board because the still all white school board believed she was a threat to the students. But like Martin, they should have let her be. So when that door of classroom 206 burst open that day, it was this kind of anxiety that embraced the thrust. I hope she wouldn't mind now but Shereva Scott said to everyone in the class to get up and get in the line with the group behind her. Poor, Mrs. Levenbrown tried to counter with "Whoever gets out of their seat will get a phone call home tonight". Now under normal situations that would have been quite enough to deter me but then Shereva recanted, "If you don't come out we will come in and get you". Something about the way she said that made me brush by Mrs. Levenbrown and head for the door. I decided that I would take my chances at home. When I got outside the classroom and saw how long the line was, I was even more impressed with my decision. Because of what happened next, it made me think about what may have happened in that room after the students left. Well, I couldn't even tell you if all the students left, because at that moment, it was about self preservation. As the line moved down the hallway busting in doors down the line I remember the students singing a song "I got the feelin', I got the feelin, I got the feeling there ain't gonna be no sh—like that." When we came down the front stairs all was in disarray.

I was told that some males jumped that big counter in the main office and beat up the Principal Mr. Hereforth and that all the white students had to be locked in the Nurses' office until they could be escorted out. Now this is sort of what shock Jock Howard Stern talks about but he got out of town before this event, I believe. I guess the intensity had been building because a few weeks earlier I was sitting in the junior high cafeteria and a fella' that I will call big brother Harrison was sitting on the cafeteria table and a teacher I shall name Mr. Parks asked him to get off the table. Well "Big brother, a member of a big family with certain reputation did not like Mr. Parks' tone. He asked "who are you talking to?" Mr. Parks responded "You, Boy!!" . . . . If you count the dots I just typed, in less time, "Big Brother was over to the other side of the table where Mr. Parks stood and punched him in the mouth. I don't know who was more shocked me or Mr. Parks. As people rushed in to observe that situation, I backed out because I didn't want to be in the position of "witness", but the riot changed the whole mind set of the district. More black teachers were hired so the district came closer to mirroring the look of its students. Black history courses were implemented. The students even won the privilege of a "smoking lounge" for the "Seniors". A couple of years later Ms. Moore did get her job back and the relocation of the Central Administration eliminated the space where the smoking lounge was located. But if I may preface the courses on Black History, I would have to relate my disappointment nationally to the way our leaders have tried to make our history as important as mainstream societies' history. As a child I remember the great efforts fought in order to have black history courses taught in public school. There was a need for our people to further our knowledge beyond a quick study of reformers, inventors and sports figures as well as a need to educate society as a whole.

That fight was basically won. Then we fought to make the month of February, "Black History" month. Well society was smart enough to figure it out that they could mount some bogus celebration during February and do away with the courses. Then, no disrespect to Stevie Wonder, we supplied great effort towards honoring Dr. Martin Luther King Jr.'s birthday as a national holiday. Now the media and the whole country publicly honors one day. I grew up in a proud "Black "town who has celebrated a lot of "Black" history months but the last few celebrated in this predominantly "Black town/school district was short of embarrassing. The most challenging situation of all was recently under an Hispanic principal, the majority holiday (Black History Month) was basically ignored or given symbolic reverence. A short time later, during a Hispanic celebration, a stringed quartet traveled the building all day playing nothing but Spanish folk music. This was in 2003 but our past is filled with these kinds of events.

I must tell you though, few people in this town fight a fight with such zeal and determination as Ms. Moore. She has even fought with Rev. Sharpton and others across the state and nation. Budget votes are her specialty. When Coretta Scott King passed, she drove all the way to Atlanta because she believed it was her responsibility to be there.

Ms. Moore has had been a mentor and Tennis coach in the community for 40 years. Her summer program has existed in Roosevelt Park (Rev Mackey). Many have gone on to do great things with their lives. I was one of Ms. Moore's first tennis students. That is how I beat Dr. J, remember?

Garney Gary

If I remember correctly I met Garney or "G" sometime in the early seventies. We were teammates on a traveling basketball team that went to Buffalo NY to play in a tournament. We also played together on the JV and Varsity Basketball squad. Although I do recall him scoring 28 points against Valley Stream North High school, he most impressed me as a skilled catcher in baseball and a brass nails linebacker and center on the football field. He played PBC football with some of my teammates and he was a heck of a long snapper for punts and field goals as well. At 150 he was the anchor of a line that averaged 225lbs. Even more impressive he was a defensive player who loved to hit people. With him Charlie Mahoney and Ron Swint behind me I was able to take certain chances at my position on the line because I knew I could trust their skills.

When we graduated he was already quite sure of his future in communications. He did not even let the fire at the school he was attending, Graham Junior College, deter him from his goal. He has had a long tenure of employment with CSPAN as a camera man and production specialist. He has represented Roosevelt well while working many important news events and most recently he was behind the camera for the Obama-McCain final debate at Hofstra University.

Garney forwarded a statement to friends and family stating. "News photographer for C-SPAN-TV. I am currently covering the Presidential Election. I am preparing for the Inauguration Ceremony in Washington, DC. I will be the cameraman shooting the head on camera at the swearing in ceremony. I will also be covering the Inaugural Balls. I am so blessed to be a member of the Press that will cover this Historic event." Raymond Mattry sent me an email one day that read: "The man said he will be shooting the head on camera at the swearing in ceremony. That's a Funk Brothers of Motown pitch for us. In other words people, Roosevelt is a major part of the history about to be made. Can you understand the words that are coming out of my mouth? So, when you pop the cork for Obama, make sure you pop the cork for Garney Gary from Roosevelt.

Now go to his page and show your love. Obama may be the first African American President, but he couldn't have done without someone from Roosevelt. Now teach the children that as well and let the record reflect.

Got anything to add, cause I'm HAPPY RIGHT ABOUT NOW. GLORY BE TO GOD!!!!." Garney is a trailblazer and therefore recognized in this historical account.

Hank Boxley and Keith Boxley

Most of my association with Hank Boxley came through sports as well. He was a first baseman in baseball and a split end/wide receiver on the football team. He was one of the people behind the creation of WRYC which was a local radio station housed inside the Roosevelt Youth Center on Mansfield Ave. During high school Hank began his career as a Mobile Disk—jockey. He was the force behind the Spectrum crew. He always had vision as I had occasion or two to hang out in the "basement" of there home "in the production studio". At first there were the school dances, house parties and weddings etc. and as the empire started to grow you would see the crew's name on billboards and posters everywhere. Younger brother Keith started to carry more of the spinning duties and before you knew it they were battling some group named Spectrum II at C.W. Post College. I do remember partying upstairs with them one time but soon the crew was in "the pit" where the top group played. The "White Van" was beginning to be known around the island. The van was also a source of humor back then because of its record of breaking down.

While in college I became a radio DJ and then did some mobile local stuff basically around campus, but not like my "homies" so I contrived my first major event, to get Spectrum to Colgate University. Nothing like that had ever happened on campus before. They had recording artist in the past but never a DJ crew. I somehow convinced the student association to fund the project and moved towards promoting the event. We had gone up to a thousand watts of FM stereo power which was big for a central N.Y. college in the seventies. I created a commercial spot that played 24 hours a day and could be heard up to forty miles from campus.

Originally this event was supposed to be in the student union, in the middle of campus, in the Main dining hall. The event then got bumped to the hockey rink for a "more popular event". The ice was removed and cooler turned down. All was set and then the day of the event I was told that the lights had to remain on even though there was a light show planned, due to "safety concerns". If I didn't agree the event would be cancelled. The show went on and the presentation was a success but the lights were an issue all night. By the time I came back from school the crew had already begun to prove that the Hip-Hop phenomenon was not just a fad. A name change to Public Enemy and an introduction to Russell Simmons and other key people and the rest is history. As the group developed the Bomb Squad went their own direction. Hank and Keith have done film soundtracks to some major movies as well as worked with and produced of number of big artists. These brothers and the Gary (Garney) family were close growing up and their trailblazing work has also represented Roosevelt well.

Patrick Curtis

Back when I was around 12 years old, I had to ride on my bike to Nassau Road quite often to get diapers for my little brother. Back then Washington Avenue went all the way through to Nassau Road. There was a drugstore at the southeast corner that my mother was comfortable with. This drugstore also served as a landmark when giving directions to our house, to family members. Before the town accessed the land across from Washington—Rose school there was deli, Mr. Curtis' Deli. Mr. Curtis, the earliest Caribbean store owner in town was well liked by the kids. If you were a little short on your transaction he worked with you and he basically gave away penny candy. Yeah! penny candy. Those were great days because I could get a bag of Wise (Onion or Barbecue) chips, a pack a Twinkies and a soda with a dollar and get change. Many times during this project I have been totally amazed by God's timing. For example, I felt I needed to speak with the gentleman by the name of Patrick Curtis. I know his son Norvel well and I had called him to see if he could arrange a meeting. We could never seem to be on the same page and then one day I was returning from a run to the store and I saw this older gentleman supporting himself on my fence taking a break. He had recent hip surgery and was probably pushing himself to hard but had chosen this time to take a little pressure of the hip. I recognized the face it was Mr. Curtis. I immediately began to ask questions. He recognized my face and Him say "Da babies, One of da babies grow up!!" in his rich Jamaican accent. I asked him how it was that he loved the kids so much, he told me that he was the second child of twelve, which made him and the older sibling responsible for clothing and feeding the under siblings. He also said that he had moved a lot in his lifetime until he settled on the store and the town. Well the "da babies" Thank you Mr. Curtis

Jackie Sinton

Earlier I wrote about a woman who contacted me from Jamestown, NY. She is the only person who I know actually was born in Roosevelt, on Bennett Avenue. She is the sister-in-law of Charles McIllwain and she was kind enough to send me the following data. These images take us back to a few through things going on in our community as early as the 1940's.

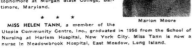

Some of Our Youth Group Members

MISS MARION MOORE, a member of the Class of 1958, Freeport High School, is one of five girls to receive a Gold Key, the highest girls' athletic award. She is also treasurer of the Girls' Athletic Association. Miss Moore plans to train for an accounting career at Brown's Business School.

* * *

MISS JACKIE WATKINS, a member of Utopia Community Centre, Inc., is now a sophomore at Morgan State College, Baltimore, Maryland.

* * *

MISS HELEN TANN, a member of the Utopia Community Centre, Inc., graduated in 1956 from the School of Nursing at Harlem Hospital, New York City. Miss Tann is now a nurse in Meadowbrook Hospital, East Meadow, Long Island.

Marion Moore

* * *

ALBERT HAYNES, a member of the Utopia Community Centre, Inc., is a graduate of Hofstra College. Now attending the University of Iowa, Iowa City, Iowa.

* * *

JOELYN SINTON is a junior at Livingstone College, Salisbury, North Carolina, where she is majoring in Social Science. She is a member of the Utopia Community Centre, Inc. She is a member of the AKA Sorority, Y.W.C.A., Spanish Club, College Choir and Concert Choir. She was chosen to be "Sweetheart of Alpha Phi Fraternity" in 1957, and was "Miss Livingstone 1956."

* * *

MISS JANICE LEFTENANT is vice president of the Library Club at Freeport High School, and is a member of the Class of 1958.

* * *

GEORGE HAYES, a former Boy Scout, is now entering the ministerial field. He will attend Lynchburg Theological Seminary at Lynchburg, Virginia.

Some of Our Youth Group Members

MISS JACQUELINE SINTON is a sophomore at Livingstone College, in Salisbury, North Carolina, majoring in Social Science. A member of Utopia Community Centre, she was the Queen of the 1957 Membership Drive. She is a member of the AKA Sorority, Spanish Club, Y.W.C.A., Women's A. A., Coleige Choir, Concert Choir, Cheerleader and Honor Student.

* * *

MISS MAXINE GILLESPIE, a member of the Utopia Youth Group, was a winner of two awards at Red Rose Cotillion, sponsored by the N.A.A.C.P. at the Waldorf Astoria Hotel in New York City on last May 31st. She is now a student at Morgan State College in Baltimor Maryland.

Jacqueline Sinton

* * *

MISS ARLENE GILLESPIE, another of our Utopia Youth Group members, is now attending Freedman's Nursing School at Howard Universi in Washington, D. C. She has also won several awards.

* * *

MISS SHIRLEY MEREDAY, former Utopia Youth Group member, w voted "Miss Transit" for 1958 by the Transit System of New York Cit Miss Mereday is a secretary and does professional modeling.

* * *

MISS SANDRA HICKS, a member of the Class of 1958, Freeport Hi School, is one of five girls to receive a Gold Key, which is the highe girls' athletic award. She is vice-president of the Girls' Athletic A sociation and one of the few student leaders in Freeport High Scho It is her ambition to be a psychologist and she plans to attend Vi ginia State College. Miss Hicks is also secretary and treasurer of t Senior Girls' Chorus.

* * *

MELVIN FOWLER, an outstanding athlete in the Class of 1958 Freeport High School, has received a scholarship to Hofstra College.

Charles R. McIlwain

C HARLES R. MCILWAIN attended primary, elementary and secondary schools in North Carolina. He obtained a Bachelor of Science degree with a major in Mathematics and a minor in Biology from Livingstone College, Salisbury, North Carolina. He received a Master of Arts degree in Educational Administration from Hofstra University, Hempstead, New York and completed further study at the University of Massachusetts at Amherst. Upon graduation from Livingstone College (1959), he served as a teacher of Mathematics at Northwest Junior High School in Charlotte, North Carolina.

Mr. McIlwain served the Roosevelt School District proudly for thirty-nine years in various positions. He began teaching Mathematics at the Roosevelt Junior-Senior High School in 1960 (first African American academic teacher). He served as Assistant Principal for six years at the Roosevelt Junior-Senior High School and as Principal of Centennial Avenue Elementary School (Roosevelt) from 1976-1996. During his tenure in Roosevelt, he served as Junior Varsity and Varsity Basketball and Junior Varsity Football Coach. Further, he coordinated instructional programs and projects to meet the academic, social, emotional, cultural, and physical needs of students. He served as the Founder and Director of the Roosevelt MAX Project for Gifted and Talented students; a highly creative, interdisciplinary, archival research project which integrates United States Civil War History and the role of African American soldiers into the teaching areas of English Language Arts, Social Studies, Math, Science, Technology and Performing Arts for 75 student in grades 4-8 with 12 superior staff members. MAX travels have included Washington, D.C., Charleston, South Carolina, Detroit, Michigan, Philadelphia, Pennsylvania, Canada, Ghana, West African and much more.

In his retirement, Mr. McIlwain continued community service work as an elected member and Chairman of the Roosevelt Citizen Advisory Council, Director of the Roosevelt MAX Project, Vice-Chairman of the Hempstead Boys and Girls Club, Member of the Roosevelt High School Advisory Committee and Bethel A.M.E. Church Bible Institute Advisory Board. He has served as Math instructor at Hofstra University, Columbia University and Long Island University and C.W. Post Campus. He is presently serving as the Program Coordinator for Roosevelt HEVN (Help End Violence Now) Cluster Program.

Mr. McIlwain is married to Joelyn Sinton McIlwain, has 3 married daughters (Alicia, Monica, and Deidre), and six brilliant, high achieving grandchildren (James, Jared, Jo'Lai, Kennedi, Jalen, and Zachary). Having received numerous awards and honors including the Lifetime Achievement Educator's Award, Livingstone College National Alumni Association, he continues to strive daily to become closer and closer to God for purpose and clarity is Mr. McIlwain's greatest honor, achievement or award.

Dr. Phillip M. Smith

Educational Excellence

Dr. Phillip M. Smith was raised in West Virginia. He obtained a Bachelor of Science degree with a major in zoology and minors in mathematics and chemistry from West Virginia State College, a Master of Arts degree in Secondary Science Education from City University of New York and a Doctorate in Education Administration from the University of Massachusetts at Amherst.

Dr. Smith served the Roosevelt School District for twenty-six years. He began teaching science and health at the Roosevelt Junior Senior High School in 1966. He served as Assistant Principal for nine years and as Principal of the Roosevelt Junior Senior High School from 1979 to 1988. During his early tenure in the Roosevelt School District, he served as Director of the Adult Education and Reading Programs; coordinator of a Multi-Level Continuous Progress Alternative Program and Principal of a Summer Reading and Math Program. Dr. Smith retired from the District after serving as District Director of Supporting Services from 1988 to 1992.

In his retirement, he continued community services as an elected member of the Uniondale School Board and served as president for several years. He is currently a trustee on the Board of Five Towns College, Dix Hills, NY, and President of the Executive Board of PLUS Group Homes for the Developmentally Disabled, Wantagh, NY. He is also a member of the Advisory Board of the international human resource firm that specializes in career management in New York City and Melville, NY.

Dr. Smith maintains membership in The National Association of Secondary Schools Principals (NAASP); The School Administrators Association of New York State (SAANYS), and The National Association of Black School Educators (NABSE). For approximately eight years he was a member of the Nassau-Suffolk School Boards Executive Committee. He served on the Financial, Legislative Committees and the State Legislative Network. Dr. Smith was recently nominated to fill a vacant seat on the New York State Board of Regents.

He is listed in: Who's who among students in American Colleges and Universities, Who's who in American Education and Who's who among Black Americans. He is a member of the NAACP and a life member of Kappa Alpha Psi Fraternity.

Dr. Smith's favorite quote is: "Schools should be safe havens. They must ensure a safe, clean, wholesome, orderly, academic environment where teachers can teach and students can learn from a diverse course of study which help individuals realize their full potential."

Dr. Phil Smith is the sole reason for my giving service to the Roosevelt School District.

In January 1981 he insisted that my time could be well spent in Roosevelt instead of Wall Street. I had graduated Colgate University with and Economics degree. I was probably more in trained in Analytical thinking. Such a quality was sure to keep in trouble at Roosevelt. Pretty much, over the years, you did what you were told to do because the thinking and planning has already been done. Dr. Smith encouraged you to be innovative.

All turns out that most of my colleagues who were headed for those pre-determined management Trainee programs would visit me in the mailroom with the rest us people of color. Analyzing my potential check against a LIRR monthly ticket it was a "no brainer" I had experienced Dr. Smith as an Assistant Principal while a student so I developed a quick working relationship.

Marion P. Fleming

Biography

Marion P. Fleming, the eldest child of Roosevelt and Theresa Parker, native Virginians who moved to Rich Square, North Carolina when she was five, became infused with the importance of education at a very early age. Supported by parents who would not permit her to fail, teachers who espoused excellence, aunts and cousins who were school teachers, and a community where the church and school were the two most important institutions, she excelled.

Graduating from the W.S. Creecy High School in 1948 as class valedictorian, she entered Hampton Institute in Hampton, Virginia where she graduated cum laude, receiving a Bachelor of Science Degree in Secondary Education. Later she received a Master of Arts Degree from Hofstra University in Hempstead, New York. In addition, she completed Post Graduate Studies at Hofstra University and New York University in New York City. Throughout all of her training she was blessed to have caring and nurturing teachers who stressed the importance of acquiring as much knowledge as possible and imparting it to others.

In 1952 she began her long career as an educator at the Huntington High School in Newport News, Virginia determined to dedicate herself to transmitting "hope and possibility" to every student who crossed her path. She subsequently organized a kindergarten in Straubing, Germany in 1957. During the same period she taught non commissioned army officers who were required to pass a proficiency test or have their service terminated. All of her students passed! Returning to the Unites States she taught at the I.C. Norcom High School in Portsmouth, Virginia and after relocating to New York, accepted a position at the North Junior High School in Brentwood, New York in 1961.

In 1965 Mrs. Fleming joined the faculty of the Roosevelt Jr.-Sr. High School in Roosevelt, New York where she remained for twenty-five years. There she served as a classroom teacher, English Department Chair, Adult Education teacher, Administrative Supervisor, and Assistant Principal. During that time some of her many activities included the development of a curriculum for the English Department which included some focus on black literature, organizing mini-courses for twelfth graders, and teaching Project Advance, a high school/college articulation program through Syracuse

University. Whatever the title, however, Mrs. Fleming was first and foremost a mentor to students in her charge.

Throughout her years at Roosevelt, Marion was also active outside her own school district. She held teaching positions at SUNY/Farmingdale, Hofstra University [the Institute for Teachers of the Disadvantage], Baldwin Summer High School, The Riverdale Children's Association and Nassau Community College. In addition, other professional activities included membership on the English Regents Question Committee in Albany, New York; the Commission on Composition for the English Council of New York State; Service on Middle States Evaluation Teams and a presenter at several annual conferences of the National Council of Teachers of English.

One of her major interests has always been the study of black history and literature. Not only did she voluntarily teach black history at her church but also spoke to various groups. The audience have been varied and extended over a wide area to include Bell Telephone workers, women's clubs, students in Long Island high schools, and at conferences sponsored by the Education Department of New York State. Perhaps the most challenging event was an assemblage of Family Court Judges in Nassau County. Regardless of the audience, however, the experiences have provided an opportunity to let others know of our history and to give a message of hope and the possibility of a better future.

Retiring from Roosevelt in July, 1990 Marion Fleming already has a new job. She spent the next nine years at Five Towns College in Dix Hills, New York where she taught English and introduced a course in African-American History. She currently teaches at Nassau Community College in Garden City, New York.

Much of her time is spent volunteering with several organizations. In 1995 she became an instructor with the AARP Defensive Driving Program, 55 Alive. In 2000, she was promoted to the position of Trainer. Her primary function is to train all instructors who teach the classes in Nassau County, but she has traveled to Westchester, Staten Island, Brooklyn and Suffolk County when needed. In 2004 she was one of the 13 volunteers across the country chosen to develop a new workbook for the program which was re-titled the AARP Driver Safety Program. Two years ago she was honored as the Amazing Driver Safety Volunteer for New York State.

Responding to a request to attend a Black History program at Cicculo de la Hispanidad, Mrs. Fleming has become greatly involved in the "Awakenings" program sponsored by Circulo and the Hofstra University

Center for Non-Violence. The purpose of this program is to tell the story of the Civil Rights Movement and provide a forum where both young and old can enter a dialogue and ultimately inspire everyone, especially youth, to continue the struggle for equal rights.

In addition, she serves as Voter Service Chair of the Central Nassau Chapter of the League of Women Voters where she moderates political debates, arranges candidate forums, conducts voter registration drives and works with the Speakers Bureau.

An active member of the Union Baptist Church in Hempstead, New York Mrs. Fleming served the youth for many years as co-youth director. She currently teaches Sunday school, and serves on the Deaconess Board and the Board of Christian Education.

Mrs. Fleming and her husband, LeRoy have been married for fifty-three years and are the proud parents of three daughters—Cheryl, Patricia, and Sandra. Their family is completed by their son-in-law Phillip, and their two grand children—Malik and Myla Sapp.

Through the years Mrs. Fleming has received many awards, but the greatest awards are those she receives daily, weekly, monthly when she meets her former students and discovers what wonderful citizens they have become. To hear the whispered "Thank you" or "I don't know where I would be if it had not been for you," gives credence to a promise she made so many years ago to give hope and possibility to every student who crossed her path.

I remember the experience of knowing Mrs. Fleming quite well. One thing I realized early on is she had very little time to play. When she was an administrator many times hallway encounters with students would leave her with such a befuddled look on her face because the students somehow did not realize that they were in a learning environment. Certain behavior on the part of the students made her question their seriousness. A student not having something to write with brought this look as well.

The story that we most revisit in our home was when I had written a paper for a class while attending Colgate University and received a B+ for a grade. My brother had Mrs. Fleming at the time and he had a major paper due. He decided that he would use the paper I wrote. I told him that Mrs. Fleming was to smart for that but he insisted that he would have one of his friends to edit and rewrite the paper and he would be fine. Mrs. Fleming returned the paper saying that she was sure that the level and subject matter on which the paper was written was not consistent with his prior work and he had to redo the paper. We all know the moral of the story and Mrs. Fleming was always good at you getting the moral. In this case it was obvious but it also proved that teachers do actually read papers.

This quote was taking from the Roosevelt Alumni Association Web site:

"A person will sometimes go through an entire lifetime without ever encountering a quality individual. Those students who attended Roosevelt Junior Senior High School were indeed fortunate to encounter a quality human being. Though her messages were sometimes philosophical and her manner very dignified, her intent was always to improve character, to instill pride and to generally promote excellence. She will forever be the Teacher's teacher, the moral conscience of our youth, the strong witted Black professional. We have shared numerous experiences with this fine lady and we wish her all the best. In recognition of your selfless dedication to the students of this school we proudly dedicate our yearbook to Mrs. Marion Fleming. May God bless you and forever keep you safe. WE the Class of 1990 say Thank you."

Mrs. Fleming was the consummate teacher and to quote Mrs. "P" (my mom), "Mrs. Fleming was not only an extraordinary administrator, but she was also a compassionate friend".

Dr. Earl Mosely

Originally I had nothing written about a very valuable entity in the development of our children's educational prowess, Dr. Earl Mosely. He was essential to the fabric and foundation of the struggle to educate all children in the town of Roosevelt. I asked Dr. Phil Smith to address my deficiency in this matter. My feelings were, what bigger tribute to pay to a man than to have his colleague and friend give testimony in his behalf. After speaking with Dr. Smith he conferred with the third individual Mr. Charles McIlwain. I affectionately called these three gentlemen "Three the Hard Way" because of their fair but much disciplined approach to educating the children of Roosevelt.

Mr. MacIIwain wrote as follows:

Professional Legacy: Dr. Earl Mosely

Dr. Mosely was a proud native of Brooklyn New York. Upon graduating from high school he enlisted in the US Military, Marine Corp. and was honorably discharged with the distinguished rank of 1st lieutenant He attended Brockport College and earned a B.S. degree in Poly-Science in Elementary Education. He would later further his educational preparation by acquiring the Master's Degree from Brooklyn College and the Doctorate Degree from the University of Massachusetts.

Dr. Mosely began an illustrious career in Education as a classroom teacher at Theodore Roosevelt Elementary School (now known as Ulysses Byas) in Roosevelt New York. Earl was the first African-American teacher to serve in the Roosevelt Union Free School District. He demonstrated that he was the consummate education professional whose daily ambition was to strive for and to achieve excellence in the workplace

Exemplary Service Excellence Award—Roosevelt

* 1955-1966 Teacher—Theodore Roosevelt
  1966-1968 Special Education Teacher—Roosevelt Jr. Sr. High School
* 1968-1970 Assistant Principal—Roosevelt Jr. Sr. High School
  1970-1991 Principal Theodore Roosevelt
* 1st African American to hold such a position in Roosevelt

It is my humble belief that Earl exemplified the following motto:

"Use me lord-show me how to take Who I am, Who I want to be and What I can do and use it for a purpose greater than myself."

Earl Mosely was always an extremely prepared, confident, and caring with very high expectations from those he served. (Students, staff, parents/community).

He would always give his all for the success of everyone involved. He spoke "Truth to Power" at all levels. His number one interest and full commitment was focused on collective and individual excellence. His daily ambition also included striving for and to achieve excellence in all areas of student growth and development. The world is a better place as a result of his God-given knowledge and talented examples.

Two of his students had the following to say about him on the Alumni Website.

I have very fond memories of Mr. Mosely. I have really missed him. He was a great guide when it came to choosing colleges and also when I needed someone to talk to. Does anyone remember the paddle he had in his office? by *Michelle Taylor-Thompson*

Good memories at TR! Who remembers "Hard for you? Easy for me!" those of us that participated in the advanced algebra program??? Mr. Mosely, God rest his spirit was such an inspiration to me well beyond my years at his school. I owe so much of my foundation and fundamentals to the staff at TR that have lasted a lifetime. by *Andrea Houston-Sherard*

Seretta McKnight

After showing high levels of potential as early as sixth grade at then Theodore Roosevelt Elementary School, I remember the persona exuded by Seretta C McKnight. As she went on to excel at Roosevelt High School she impacted our class of 1976 greatly as a student/athlete as well as politically in student government.

She then followed up with a brilliant career at Syracuse University where she developed some and honed other skills which enabled her to deal with the "Big Boys" in a "Good Ole Boy" male dominated society. Not long after graduation from Syracuse she became an intricate part of the former Yankee great and Hall of Famer Dave Winfield's Foundation. She went on to work along side the Rev. Al Sharpton in battle for racial equality and the rights of the down trodden.

Ms. McKnight then began to focus on the local battlefield as she set her ideals against the equality of African-Americans in the Town of Hempstead as well as for the children of the Roosevelt School District. She sort great changes in the way the schools were managed only to be thwarted by the state of New York. It was Ms. McKnight who first brought light to the "conspiracy" and true ideology behind the education of children in Roosevelt.

Presently, Ms. McKnight is the President of the Roosevelt Kiwanis Club. She has answered a call by the "Most High" to minister to the people. Sister Minister, as she is referred to spiritually, has bridged the gap between local and community issues, educating our children, and working under the will of God. Her work has become synonymous with two organizations WHAM and Sisters of The Struggle and can be heard weekly on Thursday afternoons on WTHE 1520 AM. The history salutes this Roosevelt resident of over forty years, Ms. Seretta C. McKnight

T Schlegel

It is no coincidence that Todd has the same last name as Rudolph, the gentleman mentioned hitherto in the John Mackey story as well as in some unfavorable comments made by the first waive of African-Americans to come to Roosevelt. Where the similarities end is with the name.

Todd was a student in Roosevelt and married an African-American woman. He became and educator in Roosevelt who taught Astronomy and did a superb job of running the Planetarium. Because of my academic requirements I was not able to take his course and was disappointed by the fact that all my classmates and teammates told me he was a cool teacher. He gave you all the opportunity in the world to pass the course unlike those teachers I had for Biology, Chemistry and Physics.

Mr. Schlegel was forced to move on to a better opportunity to support his family. There was a period where all the neighboring school districts hired our teachers away with higher salaries. Oddly enough the state of the art planetarium the reason why other school districts to plan field trips to our school, was allowed to be destroyed and is now a teacher's lounge.

Whether working in Roosevelt, which he returned for a second tour or while in Uniondale, he never forgot or ignored his relationship with Roosevelt Student/Alums. He has spent a great effort to keep alumni in touch and networking by holding a function every summer at Eisenhower Park. I most remembered when Danielle Davis braided his blonde hair. I was amazed and wondered how they would stay until she brought the rubber bands out. We also salute Todd Schelgel for his years of service to this community.

MISS SHELLEY'S
UPWARD PREP

Infants • Toddlers
Pre-K • Kindergarten

66 Nassau Road
P.O. Box 603
Roosevelt, NY 11575-2034

Tel. 516-378-9206
Fax 516-378-9208

Hours of Operation
7:00 a.m. - 6:00 p.m.
Administration Office Hours
8:00 a.m. - 5:00 p.m.

ACCREDITATION

NYS Education Department
Non-Public School Recognition
NYS Children & Family Services
Day Care Center License
NYS Department of Health
NAEYC Accreditation Projected*
*(in self-study phase)

FEATURES

Innovative Experiential Curriculum
Certified and Trained Faculty
Extended Hours for Working Families
Year-Round Programs
Uniform Dress Code
Closed Circuit TV Monitoring
Meals Supplied

BACKGROUND

On April 5, 1979 the program was founded with a vision to provide low- and middle- income working families quality early childhood programs that featured affordable services targeted toward their needs: extended day programming, nutritional meals, developmentally appropriate culturally sensitive curricula, an attractive and clean facility, and a loving and disciplined family environment.

Since its founding the program has grown into a private non-profit community based institution with early childhood and intermediate education programs (Pre-K to Kindergarten); youth development; and family support programs. The program has achieved recognition from NYS Education Department as a non-public school, has had its program evaluated as "substantially equivalent in instruction" by the NYS Education Department for non-public schools, and obtained a day care center license from NYS Children and Family Services.

MISSION

The mission of the program is to provide experiential and culturally sensitive programs, curricula, and activities that foster the growth and development of moral and intellectual autonomy, within an environment that values diversity and peace.

PHILOSOPHY AND GOALS

The program's philosophy of education is based on constructivist models of education, and embodies the following principles:

- The developmental level of the learner must be respected.
- All students and teachers can learn.
- Focusing on the strengths must come first when looking at the learner.
- Teachers and adult family members must demonstrate themselves as "joyfully literate."
- Learners need many opportunities for "languaging."
- The learning process is highly valued.
- Evaluation is ongoing.
- The goal of education is interdependence.
- Learning is lifelong and requires thoughtfulness.
- The teacher is a facilitator and co-learner.
- Curriculum is negotiated, and learners have choices.
- "Demonstrations" are necessary for learning.
- Sharing is an important part of learning.
- Sufficient time is needed for optimal learning.
- Collaboration and social interaction build effective learning environments.

Our goals for each individual student who attends the program are to:

- understand themselves;
- find meaning in their world;
- construct their futures;
- adapt to change; and
- have an impact on their world.

In Memorial

9/11

I WAS LIVING in Rock Hill, South Carolina and I was home from work that day. I was watching one of those AM news shows when the camera shifted to the first plane going into the World Trade Center. This was before anyone knew what was going on. The newscaster first reported it as a simple plane crash. I even watched the clip when they showed the President being told in that elementary school classroom he was visiting in Florida. After the first day you did not see that clip anymore and I think it was quite frankly because the President did not seem to be surprised at all. I can remember feeling that it must have been some real coincidence, the way the whole scenario unfolded. Firstly, I don't care how well you play poker, the President's reaction was one of prior knowledge. Secondly, how did he happen to be in brother Jed's state when it was all going down, on his porch back in Washington. I also thought it was fishy that the greatest, most powerful country in the world was supposedly without leadership while Mr. Bush made it to the Western compound, where Presidents go when the country is under attack. Who was actually running country for those few hours when he disappeared on his route to his "safe house?" Admittingly so, all my immediate reactions dealt with governmental issues and I had not thought about the people who were turned into weapons or those more importantly who turned into human targets.

Most of the people who had been affected directly by this traumatic event had their resolve within hours but some had to wait longer until the list had been compiled. As the list unfolded, like most, I realized I too had been affected as well. One of my esteemed classmates from Colgate University, Sharon D. Balkom, a very sweet well-liked person had perished. May God grant her great peace in her eternal rest.

But then the affect came closer to Roosevelt. During my years of coaching at Roosevelt I had the opportunity to coach one Crossley Williams for Junior High Baseball. My relationship with him is memorable as we both shared an equal frustration at him being the catcher. But he was a very intelligent kid. May God continue to bless his rest as well as his family.

The next person was popular because of his ability to contain his high level of intelligence within a cool personality. Brian Jones and his brother Gary were regulars at the basketball court at Roosevelt Park. Their father is former NBA official, Lee Jones and these guys wound up moving to Dix Hills during their high school years, I believe. Brian was also at work that very sad day and perished. Gone but not forgotten! This historical account will help towards that goal. May all those who were affected by 9/11 be blessed.

(Submitted by Bro UjimaAbdullah)

(Submitted by Bro Ujima Abdullah)

6/13/07

I woke to a cloudy morning on June 13, 2007.

Four days before Father's Day and my spirit seemed a little unsettled. The Saturday before I was at a four hour homegoing celebration for the mother of one of my fellow church members and my niece had buried her father the day before. But this day! As I traveled to work I began to pray. Little did I know that when I entered the school, that morning, that the first person I would greet, would tell me that her father had been found unconscious and had to be rushed to the hospital. As Dora Staten-Smith solicited my prayers I became saddened because as she stopped to have some breakfast she said "You need to have something on your stomach when dealing with these kinds of situations". I wasn't quite clear on what that meant but again my inner spirit began to feel low. I couldn't call him my friend because I didn't know him long enough but he was very supportive of this project and came to meet twice to give me information. He even told me how hard it was to meet with me the second time because of prior obligations with his wife but "Nevertheless".

SHELDON PARRISH

You see the person she was talking about was Mr. Walter Mackey Jr. He was the only one to show up for my first interview session at VFW Post#1957. I had been experiencing some writer's block and I had not been attentive to the project but this was my very fear that someone would transition during the process, and now a reality. God Bless your life, Mr. Walter Mackey Jr. . . . .

Mackey Collection

Walter Dennis

I wasn't fortunate enough to play for Mr. Dennis because he believed in coaching at the Junior level and I was too old when we moved to town. Living across from Roosevelt Park though, many Saturday mornings I awoke to screaming and cheering from the young kids and their parents. The baseball games started at 10am. Mr. Dennis was unique in that he worked for the Town of Hempstead driving a street sweeper, but when you saw him on his way to work or with children in the community he was always walking. More interesting is that you would always see him carrying a dufflebag full of Baseball equipment. The contents of this bag usually included a few bats, balls, helmets and catcher equipment. He would carry this bag from way down on the Southside to the Town of Hempstead Depot or to Mr. Swint's (Another mentor PBC Boxing) house on East Clinton and they would ride to work together.

Another fond memory happened one summer at his son Jeffery's house. It was a summer barbecue and I had just finished cooking my well known Seafood Gumbo when Mr. Dennis and Uncle Willie, a relative of there's, decided to train me on the "proper way" to cook crabs. They laughed and teased me as they stated that I did not have the proper southern child rearing (North Carolina to be exact) to complete the task. Upon completion I enjoyed probably the tastiest crabs I ever had. Guess what? Later I found out that neither one was from North Carolina.

Mr. James Simpson

(Simpson III Collection and Roosevelt Alumni Corp)

Mr. Simpson would be in the running for the Town Most Valuable Player Award, if there was such an award. Over the years many youths turned into men with the influence of Mr. Simpson. He was an innovator for creating programs, a coach par excellence, and had direct involvement in baseball, basketball and football. I remember my first trip out town that was not family orientated was with Mr. Simpson. He, Frank Brown and Univester Smith took our team overnight to Buffalo NY for a basketball tournament. My brothers have also traveled to places like Louisiana for the Biddy Basketball Championships. Mr. Simpson will probably be mentioned in a couple places in this project but this is a statement from the Newsletter dedicated to the scholarship awarded in his name to a deserving Roosevelt student.

Jim Simpson Memorial
Scholarship Fund

On June 30, 1997, the Roosevelt community lost one of its longtime residents and community leaders, Jim Simpson. Jim's community service included being the pastor of Mount Olive Baptist Church, Medford, NY; founder, coordinator, director and member of many Roosevelt civic organizations, such as PBC, PAL, Roosevelt Coaches Association, the Joe Murphy American Legion; and an employee of Nassau BOCES. Jim was the recipient of the Roosevelt Board of Education Martin Luther King Outstanding Citizen Award. Upon his death, several of his friends, family members, neighbors and colleagues formed this fund, the Jim Simpson Memorial Scholarship Fund. We began working toward one of Jim's greatest desires, to offer the young people of this community a chance to improve their dignity, self-respect and education.

The mission of this community based organization is to encourage and support higher education among the youth of Roosevelt through its scholarship fund. Over the past nine years, the committee has been successful in doing just that. Through donations, and fund raising efforts (an Annual Gospel Fest Luncheon, plays, sport events, talent show, and an awards breakfast) we were able to award scholarships to over 30 students over the past nine years.

Jim Simpson Memorial
Scholarship Fund
P.O. Box 162
Roosevelt, NY 11575

(Photo care of Don Crummell)
Alvin F. Crummell 1918-1978

One of our true soldiers who transitioned and went to be in a better place sometime ago is Al Crummell. Al Crummell wore an expression that meant he was about business. He was a proud man and was proud of his community. But on the other side of his personality he was a very humorous individual. I always did exactly what he said because I didn't know about that funny side.

Mr. Crummell was born in Charleston South Carolina one of 5 boys and 4 girls. After graduating high school he moved to Freeport as a young man. He went on to the military and served the US Army in World Was II. After a bid overseas in 1950 he returned to purchase a home on Brooks Ave with the help of the G.I. bill for housing.

At this time, the fifties, the Southside was where African-Americans lived and Al Crummell became a force with civic groups and community organizations and with a partner his Fred Douglas, they started an African-American Society Watch Organization called the Esquires. They were involved with local politics, schools, and social functions in the Freeport/Roosevelt area. Many fundraising events were held at the Huntington Town House. There place to hold many civic meeting was the Sportsman's 30. This well known historical establishment was basically the headquarters for most civic activity. Multi-purpose in it's use, the building, was located on Babylon Turnpike just before the fork in the road, on the west side of the street.

Al Crummell got involved with the Roosevelt Little League in (1963) as he and many African-American fathers wanted their sons to play organized baseball. Leagues were all ready functioning for the white youth. The fathers, some of them you have heard mentioned hitherto, met this task with opposition but managed to get into leadership positions to fully integrate the league. The ground work that needed to be done served as glue to bond the community men like Mr. Oscar Glass, Mr. Marion Gary, Mr. Walter Dennis, Mr. Jim Simpson, Mr. Richard P Warren, Mr. Henry Aiken Sr., Luther Johnson, Elmer Bryant, Charles Dudley, George Jones, George Blackburn and many, many more. Mr. Crummell took another step in fortifying inclusion for our youth when he became a member of the newly formed Roosevelt DAD's Club in 1966.

Mr. Crummell became the first African-American President of the Roosevelt Little League in 1968. He changed the whole persona of "Opening Day" in Roosevelt making it a major happening including bands and fire trucks, it became a bigger parade than Memorial Day. Because of his hard work the local Chamber of Commerce asked him to Marshall the Memorial Day parade. The same crew mentioned early were some of the same people that worked along side and were instrumental in making the parade an instant success with other towns such as Freeport and Hempstead with the local newspapers issuing accolades.

Mr. Crummell then decided to forge further by becoming an umpire at the high school level. Another milestone for African-Americans, locally. I have to say personally that Mr. Crummell was great for kids. He was a great coach and a great example. He and Mr. Marion Gary were neighbors and both of these gentleman had such an effect on young kids lives that for almost twelve years the starting center and long range snapper of the Varsity football team came from one of their homes and if you happened to recognize the name his wife just recently retired from direct care of youth at the PAL. His son follows his legacy of civic mindedness and giving to others unselfishly. The "seed" Don Crummell has won Championships as Varsity Football Coach and as a Varsity Girls Basketball Coach. He has won countless awards for "Coach" and "Man" of the Year because he believes in the total enrichment of his student/athlete not just their sports prowess. He is the Attendance officer, Contract negotiator, advocate for families in court and so savvy in Roosevelt problem troubleshooting that I expect him to be the lead administrator at some point. It will be hard tearing him away from the coaching part because theoretically you can not do both but he is definitely qualified to run the ship.

(Gary Collection)

Mr. Marion D. Gary

Wednesday, January 24, 2007
1:00 p.m.
Friendship Missionary Baptist Church
302 Brodie Road
Batesburg-Leesville, South Carolina
Reverend James A. Duncan, Pastor Officiating

Marion Gary entered into eternal rest Saturday, January 20, 2007. He was born September 2, 1927 to the late Albert Gary and Mary Ann McDaniel.

Mr. Gary was a graduate of Ridge Spring High School, Ridge Spring, South Carolina. He entered Benedict College, Columbia, South Carolina. He was a US Army veteran having served in the Korean War. In September of 1950, he was married to Catherine Padgett.

Mr. Gary was a member of Judea Baptist Church where he was a deacon, led the Men's Choir and Feed the Hungry Committee. Mr. Gary was active in his community serving as President of the Jim Simpson Memorial scholarship Fund, coached little league baseball id midget football, member of the Long Island Empire's Association, Sergeant-at-Arms of the Roosevelt Sharpshooters, a mentor at the Police Activity League, a member of the Zion 36 M.F.M. Masonic Lodge and the American Legion-Joe Murphy Post Number 1957, Roosevelt, New York.

He leaves to cherish his memories: his wife of 56 years—Catherine P. Gary; three sons—Albert Gary and Brian Gary, both of Long Island, New York and Garney Gary of Maryland; three daughters—LaVerne Brown of Georgia and Natalie Gary-Connor and Hope Gary, both Long Island, New York; one brother—James (Thelma) Gary of Rockville Centre, New York; eight grandchildren—Tisha (Tracy), Terencia, Chanel, Chad, McKenzie, Brittany, Brian-Keith and Myles; three great-grandchildren—Gabrielle, Brianna and Derek, a host of nieces, nephews, other relatives and many sorrowing friends.

Frank Brown

Submitted by Terencia Brown

My first take on this man was that he was country as all get out. But that "southern mystique" made me grow to have much respect for him as my first coach and all-around, good person to talk to. He talked to me about curve balls and foul shots and sometimes about just trying to make it through the struggle of being a big black youth in the 70's. He was responsible for my first trip away from home. We went to Buffalo to play basketball and there were two family rules being broken by just getting in the car. First of all going that far away from home without my mother had been only a wish. Secondly, I was going to miss church on Sunday. The compromise was that my Dad went along. These days most kids wish their father had time to go along. Mr. Simpson and my father road in the station wagon with us and Coach Brown and Coach U Smith came in another vehicle.

When I grew too old to play for the leagues Coach became a fan. "I was one of his boys", of course. He followed me through high school, basketball and football and I was even honored to have the same four gentleman come to watch me play when the Red Raiders of Colgate University came into Manhattan to play Columbia University. I remember how they fussed after the game about a particular stunt technique Colgate had us using where we feathered the QB and jumped off on the pitchman on option. They were still coaching and I was just happy they were there. Needless to say, they got me in trouble the next week of practice for listening to them on a play.

The only other non-family visitors I had was the legendary Ollie Mills from Hempstead. He introduced me to his oldest son Steve. Steve was attending Princeton and they came down after the game an introduced themselves. Funny, that game was the first I played against new Princeton coach Al Pearman, the Alumni from Roosevelt, who was responsible for me being at Colgate but had since moved on.

Frank and Ollie and Don Ryan all knew each other through the ministry of giving kids a chance. A "real grass roots ministry" that did not get much respect then, but does now.

> Those who are still fighting, Keep up the fight.
> Those of you resting, you earned it.

The last time I saw Coach Brown he had flown back in town after relocating to see his friend Univester Smith, who he heard had been sick. He looked very tired and although he had not expected his friend to live, he preceded him in death.

Univester Smith

Sunrise
11/23/35

Sunset
12/1/00

(Submitted by Maurice Smith)

Wednesday,—December 6, 2000
6:00 PM
Mt. Sinai Baptist Church Cathedral
Rev. Dr. A. L. Mackey Sr. Ave
Roosevelt, NY 11575

Obituary

Univester Smith affectionately known as "Sylvester" to all who knew him. He was born to the union of Calvin Roosevelt Wright & Lillian Carroll on November 23, 1935 in Chatham County, Savannah Georgia. He departed this life on December 1, 2000.

Bro. Smith was educated in the Savannah School System. After that he enlisted in the US ARMY in 1954 and served in the Korean War. He received medals of honor namely the Korean Service Medal, The ROK Presidential Unit Citation and the National Defense medal.

In the early sixties Univester moved to Freeport with his family. He eventually also moved to Roosevelt. He was active with the Police Activity League (PAL) formerly known as the Police Boys Club (PBC) for many years before his health began to fail.

Bro. Smith was preceded in death by his brother Marion Groover of New York and his sister Gladys of Georgia. He is survived by his loving wife Viola

Smith, five children by a previous marriage Janis L. Smith of Charleston SC, Elder Michael U. Smith (Darlene) of Boston Mass, Karen M Smith of Freeport, Andre B Smith of Hempstead NY, Theodore M Smith (Karen) of Hempstead and Minister Maurice A. Smith (Stephanie) of Roosevelt NY Thirteen grandchildren and two great-grandchildren.

Henry Aiken Sr.

Mr. Aiken Sr. was also another one of those people who spent a countless number of hours mentoring and coaching kids. I have continuously said that what the generation that follows mine needs most is the impact from the kind of individual who worked so diligently from the generation before us. My generation dropped the ball. We haven't transitioned the lessons very well at all. Mr. Henry Aiken Sr. was another one of those people who worked hard during the day to provide for his family and then still always found time for the kids.

The Aiken family realized that it took many soldiers and so my good friend Henry Aiken Jr. followed in the footsteps of his father. He was also about the kids. He often volunteered to teach baseball skills to many of the youth in the community. He was a big man who didn't run very well but he wielded a bat and could place a hit baseball practically any where on the field he wished. Hank, as we affectionately called him, departed this life as a young man. He had served the class of 1977 as an officer and a gentleman and his community equally but departed in October of 1990 two weeks after my other friend Morris Brandon.

Rev. Timothy Wright

(Newsday Photos)

Roosevelt has also been the home of a family of talented Gospel singers, writers and musicians, led by the father Reverend Timothy Wright, pastor of the Grace Tabernacle Christian Center Church of God in Christ in Brooklyn, NY. While working for the school district I had the opportunity to speak with his grandson, Daniel "DJ" Wright Jr. One day as I dealing with some personal issues I began to hum and then sing lowly a song Jesus, Jesus Jesus A Recent hit from their ministry. "D.J." perked up and walked over to me and said my grandmother wrote that song.

I last saw her at a service at Greater Second Baptist Church. All I ever heard about was that sweet spirit she had. Even my mother, who had some dealings with the family at the school, had an unwavering opinion of Mrs. (Sis) Wright. That is why it was so saddening to hear what had happened on that trip back from Detroit. It seems that there were many stories about this woman and she seems to have departed before we all could get our fill of the pleasantries but God never makes mistakes and He chose to rid "D.J." and Grandma from dealing with this hellacious world we live in. God Bless the Wright Family. (Internet-Newsday)

A popular gospel singer from Roosevelt is slowly recovering from the car crash that injured him and killed his wife and grandson.

While the Rev. Timothy Wright, pastor of Grace Tabernacle Christian Center Church of God in Christ in Brooklyn, knows his grandson has died, he has not yet been told the fate of his wife and co-pastor, Betty Wright.

"He's holding on," said his son David Wright. The pastor suffered extensive injuries, including a broken jaw. "He's conscious. He can't talk, but he can nod his head."

Wright remained in critical condition yesterday at Geisinger Medical Center in Danville, Pa.

Another of the pastor's five sons Danny Wright—whose own 14-year-old son D.J. died in the crash—said his father has been asking for his wife. The family has pledged to wait to break the news until Wright is physically stronger.

The Wrights were returning from a religious convention in Detroit late on July 4 when their car was struck head-on by another car driving the wrong way on Interstate 80 in Pennsylvania.

D.J., who died from his injuries on Saturday night, had just graduated eighth grade from Roosevelt Middle School. He loved cooking and the Power Rangers, and he wanted to be a gospel singer like his grandfather.

(Newsday Photo)

"He was a perfect kid," said his mother, Lori Wright, before dissolving into tears. "Not an ounce of trouble. He loved gospel music, he loved all types of music. You couldn't ask for the more perfect child."

The trip to Detroit with his grandparents was a special graduation present for D.J., one of the couple's three sons, Danny Wright said.

"I never really let them away from us, but he wanted to go," Danny Wright said. He said he spoke to his son every day during the trip, and had just talked with him hours before the crash.

The next time he saw D.J., "he looked like himself, like he was just sleeping," Wright said. "He probably didn't even know what happened."

Copyright © 2008, Newsday Inc.

* This section was written before Reverend Timothy Wright's transition and I hope God truly blesses his journey and the reunion between the three great spirits that road in the truck that day from Detroit.

Melvin C. Walker

A42 **OBITUARIES**

LONG ISLAND

The Rev. Melvin Walker, 70, gospel radio host

BY SID CASSESE
sid.cassese@newsday.com

The Rev. Melvin C. Walker, a gospel radio personality who was dubbed "The Gospel Ambassador" by radio legend Joe Bostic and was a force for aiding victims of natural disasters, died last Thursday at Winthrop University Hospital in Mineola after a brief illness. The Hempstead resident was 70.

Walker, a gospel promoter whose family said helped many of today's most widely known performers, also had been pastor of the Gospel Blessing Center on Nassau Road in Roosevelt until his retirement in 2001.

"During the 1970s, many well-known groups — such as the Walter Hawkins Singers, The Winans and the Clark Sisters — had their first appearance in New York as a result of his promotions," said his son Robert Walker of Mastic Park.

To Long Islanders, though, Walker was best known for his gospel radio shows and his efforts to help victims of natural disasters.

"He was a leader among ministers in raising awareness and money for those caught in tragic circumstances, especially from natural disasters. And his radio shows brought words of inspiration to many Long Islanders,"

Parishioners led by the Rev. Melvin Walker, right, distribute food, warm clothing and blankets.

pastor of Memorial Presbyterian Church in Roosevelt.

"He did more to keep gospel alive than any other person I know," said his friend, the Rev. Al Sharpton. "And there was not a major event in my life, whether in civil rights or the ministry, when I did not ask him to be involved. It wasn't important unless Melvin Walker was there."

from Philadelphia in 1962, following the trucking company for which he drove. In 1964 he parlayed his love of gospel music into a job as artist and repertoire director for Holi-Scepter Records in Manhattan. It was during this time that Bostic, the late dean of gospel disc jockeys and the first black American radio announcer, dubbed Walker "The Gospel Ambassador."

recording studio in Brooklyn, where he lived. About 1971, he shifted to a music store in Brooklyn, but still did promotions. He closed the store in 1978.

In 1981, Walker took over the old Highway Inn Night Club on Nassau Road in Roosevelt, near the Southern State Parkway. There he did music promotions and evangelical revivals. In 1984 he graduated from the Commu-

and became pastor of the Gospel Blessing Center, and in 1985, he received an honorary doctorate degree from National Theological Seminary of the Commonwealth University in St. Louis.

From 1972 onward, Walker, off and on, hosted a gospel radio show.

After retiring in 2001, Walker moved to a senior complex in Hempstead and remained active.

The Rev. Milton E. Rochford in Hempstead said that just last month he and Walker got permission to have two concerts at the county jail, for men in August and for women in December. He said they will now be held in Walker's honor.

In addition to his son, Walker is survived by his wife of 49 years, Shirley; four other sons, David of Wheatley Heights, Steven of Philadelphia, Melvin Jr. of Hempstead and John of Townsends, Del.; two daughters, Yvonne Curtis of Philadelphia and Sharnel Wiggs of Randallstown, Md.; and 10 grandchildren.

Viewing will be from 4 to 7 p.m. tomorrow at Zion Cathedral in Freeport, followed by a Joy Night Service from 7 to 11 p.m. On Saturday, viewing will be from 9 to 10 a.m., followed by the funeral at 10 a.m. Burial will follow at Pinelawn Ceme-

---

In the eighties a man by the name of Melvin C. Walker bought the old HYWAY Inn on Nassau Road at the corner of East Raymond and started church called the Blessing Center. Rev Walker had already claimed fame by being a radio personality. He was known as the "Gospel Ambassador" on WTHE an Am station for Gospel music. My reflection is that in the Spring of 1976 I had the opportunity to do his show. Rev Walker had to leave town for a week and he turned the reigns over to my pastor, the Rev. E. Mitchell Mallette (Greater Second Baptist Church, Freeport). Rev. Mallette asked me to go along with him to read the "Prayer List" and announcements. That small experience led to my interests in radio and I wound up subbing for some of the Disc-jockeys on the air at my college WRCU (Colgate University) that summer. I did so well that I became the first freshman to have a radio show the first semester (Fall). This was the obituary in Newsday.

The Five Churches mentioned by Harry D. Daniels
as submitted by those churches

The Five Churches as submitted by church officers:

HISTORY OF **MT. SINAI BAPTIST CHURCH**
243 Frederick Avenue,
Rev. Dr. A. L. Mackey, Sr., Avenue
Roosevelt, New York 11575

THE LATE REV. Walter R. Mackey, Sr. always said, "God gave me a divine vision and I saw the Mt. Sinai Baptist Church full of people serving God long before I ever set foot in this neck of the woods."

It was from that divine inspiration that gave birth to the Mount Sinai Baptist Church, which started as a Mission on Labor Day, 1949 with five (5) members. They were Dora Mackey, Walter Mackey, Larry Mackey, Annette Haynes and Eddy Walker. Four nights of service followed with a different Church each night and their pastor. On Sunday, October 23, 1949, two additional members joined, Arthur Mackey and John Mackey bringing the total to seven (7) members. In the basement of 216 Manhattan Avenue, Roosevelt, New York, the Rev. Walter R. Mackey organized the Mt. Sinai Baptist Church.

Mrs. Dora Mackey, wife of Rev. Walter R. Mackey, was the first Usher and first Missionary President. Mrs. Carrie Starapoli volunteered her services by offering to play for the church, **free of charge**. A choir was then organized, with Mrs. Carrie Starapoli as Organist and Mrs. Dora Mackey, President of the Choir.

From July 1St to July 13th, 1951, a Revival was held on the present site, in a tent 30 **X** 60 feet. Rev. Dr. W. C. Evans was the Revivalist and the Hatcher Singers of Brooklyn, New York furnished the music. Eleven (11) members were added to the church; six were candidates for Baptism.

Due to the increase in membership, larger quarters were necessary to house the congregation. In 1951, from the land acquisition to the brick front and the cross-toppled steeple, Mount Sinai Baptist Church was built almost single handed by the Late Walter R. Mackey, Sr.

On the fourth Sunday in August 1952, the members marched from 216 Manhattan Avenue to the basement of the present site. Services were conducted in the basement for one (1) year. On the fourth Sunday in August of 1952, the members marched upstairs. There were a faithful few who assisted Rev. Mackey in the struggle to build the edifice for God. In August 1955, a tired but happy and proud, Rev. Walter R. Mackey preached the first sermon in the Mt. Sinai Baptist Church.

The Late Rev. Dr. Arthur L. Mackey, Sr. became the pastor after his father retired. Rev. Dr. Mackey would always say, "If I can help somebody, then my living will not be in vain." Rev. Mackey was well known throughout the community, state and even the nation. He worked as a Community Relations Specialist for Nassau County Commission on Human Rights and later as the Director of Nassau County Job Development Program. He was the first Black Chairman of the Trustee Board at the Nassau County Medical Center. He negotiated with Governor Cuomo to institute the Open Heart Program. His affiliations, committees and involvements span the United States and are too vast and numerous to list. However, he loved most being involved where he could help people.

It was the vision of Dr. Mackey, which founded the "I Support Roosevelt Youth Center." The center was formerly a Jewish Synagogue and School. The church purchased the property and the vision to find a way and a place to help the youth and community to grow.

Under the leadership of Rev. Dr. A. L. Mackey, Sr., many ministries were formed. He also installed three of the church's faithful members as the first female trustees—Mrs. Mary E. Portis, Mrs. Vivian (Mackey) Smith and Mrs. Margaret Thompson.

On October 29, 1999, Rev. Dr. Arthur L. Mackey, Sr., departed this life after a brief illness and his only son, Rev. Arthur L. Mackey, Jr. was installed as pastor.

Today, the Mt. Sinai Baptist Church is actively involved with the leaders of the Youth Center. The Center has been restored and beautified. It now houses the Roosevelt Children's Academy. Many youth programs and outreach programs are serving the community. We are growing and expanding in our vision. At the church, we continue to beautify the sanctuary. In the last seven years, we have expanded the church fifty (50) feet and renovated the lower level.

The Good Shepherd Story

Foundations

While the Lutheran Church of the Good Shepherd, Roosevelt, New York, was officially organized as a parish in 1949, Lutherans who lived in Roosevelt had traveled to Christ Church, Freeport, for many years before they had their own church. By 1931, two buses were transporting church school pupils from Roosevelt to Freeport every Sunday morning. In that year, the Rev. David G. Jaxheimer, pastor of Christ Church, proposed to the church council that a branch Sunday school be started in Roosevelt. The plan had the support of the United Lutheran Synod of New York and New England.

By a margin of one vote, the Freeport council approved the proposal. The Square Club Hall on Babylon Turnpike and Centennial Avenue was rented for $20 a month. On Sept. 13, the first church school sessions were held but only 17 attended due to a measles epidemic. Subsequent growth justified the venture, for the school was soon fully staffed and enrollment gradually increased until in 1948 it stood at 180.

After several years, the Square Club's membership had decreased substantially. They offered Christ Church ownership of the hall if the church would assume a mortgage of $4,000 and responsibility for an accumulation of unpaid bills. At the time, banks were not lending money to churches without personal guarantees. For the purchase of the Roosevelt property, the sum of $700 was needed, and Dr. Jaxheimer became the personal guarantor. (The loan was repaid in less than a year.) Title to the Square Club property was assumed on March 30, 1943, and it was renamed Christ Lutheran Chapel.

Parish Beginnings

Officially organized with 80 charter members on February 23, 1949, the congregation adopted the name, Lutheran Church of the Good Shepherd, and elected its first church council. Incorporation followed on April 19. A call was extended to Charles D. Trexler, Jr., a senior at Lutheran Theological Seminary, Mt. Airy, Philadelphia, to become the pastor. He accepted the call on April 30, to take effect on June 1. He was ordained by the synod on June 15, 1949.

Although the history of Pastor Trexler's family reads like a" Who's Who" in the Lutheran Church, his personal story was also notable at the time he became Good Shepherd's pastor. He was a Princeton University contemporary of Jimmy Stewart and Jose Ferrer who graduated cum laude and was Ivy Day orator at the commencement exercises in 1935. Later he became a Broadway actor, associated with such stars as Cornell Wilds, Brook Pemberton and Ethel Barrymore. When World War II broke out, he enlisted in the U.S. Army as a private, rising to the rank of lieutenant colonel, and helping to plan the invasion of North Africa. After the war, he heard the call to the Holy Ministry, as had his father, uncles and grandfather before him. This was the man called to lead the Roosevelt flock. Pastor Trexler's installation was on September. 25, 1949, at Christ Church, Freeport,

A Decade of Rapid Growth

Highlights of 1952 included organization of the Brothers of the Good Shepherd, the men's club, and the first vacation Bible school. In November, the congregation purchased a house and property adjoining the chapel for $22,000. This was renovated into a rectory for the pastor and a parish house with eight classrooms. The church now owned the entire block front on Babylon Turnpike between Centennial Ave. and Allers Blvd.

On April 19, 1953, the parish house was dedicated by the Rev. Eugene Kreider, mission superintendent. In October, a weekday school with an enrollment of over 100 children was begun under the released time law of the State of New York. In December, a children's bell choir was organized, one of the first in Lutheran churches in America.

The year of 1954 was marked by the congregation assuming the entire amount of the pastor's salary. The fifth anniversary of the parish's founding was celebrated on Good Shepherd Sunday, May 2, followed by an anniversary dinner on May 7 at the South Shore Yacht Club, Freeport, with 325 in attendance. A $6,000 mortgage was burned, a 1954 Mercury sedan was presented to Pastor Trexler and an anniversary book was published. A preaching mission in October, with Pastor von Schenk again the missioner, drew an average of 234 persons to each of the five services.

On November 27, 1955 the final mortgage on the church property was burned by Mrs. Barbara Jaeger, oldest member of the congregation. The church was then debt free and no longer on mission status but a fully independent parish.

Toward a New Church

During the spring of 1956, a study of Good Shepherd's building needs was begun with assistance of the ULCA's Department of Church Architecture. The rapid growth of the parish had quickly made the little chapel building inadequate. A building committee was appointed, headed by William C. Andrews. In October, a building fund drive for $150,000 began with the assistance of Lawson Associates, professional fundraisers.

At a congregational meeting in June 1958, it was voted to buy land, on Brookside Avenue between Centennial and Hudson Avenues. Reasons for the move included the increasing commercialization of Babylon Turnpike and the need for more off street parking because of a Town of Hempstead ordinance requiring such facilities for public buildings. Title to part of the property was taken in October 1958, and the remainder in January 1959. Meanwhile, Pastor Trexler had been named president of the Long Island Conference, which involved frequent absences to consult with other congregations and for synod meetings. Along with the rapid growth of Good Shepherd, this extra responsibility for the pastor dictated the wisdom of calling an assistant pastor for the parish.

A Decade of Building

The 1960s were a time of many changes in the world, in the country, in Roosevelt and in the Church of the Good Shepherd. For the church, the first half of the decade was a time of building, both spiritual and material, on the foundations laid during its first ten years.

The major building project was the construction of the new church Designed by T. Norman Mansell of Philadelphia, the contemporary style church, seating 290, cost about $200,000. Ground breaking was held August 7, 1960 and excavation began in October. By the following April the date stone was ready to be laid. General contractor for the project was Gundersen Construction Co. William C. Andrews chaired the building committee through the years of planning and construction. Dedication day was October 1, 1961. A two-and-one-half hour service was preceded by a procession of 600 members and friends from Centennial Ave. School, led by the church council and clergy.

The congregation had, of course, left behind the old church property on Babylon Turnpike, though the pastors continued to live in the parish house there. By May, 1962, the old property was sold to the African Methodist Episcopal Zion Church, and in September the pastors moved to temporary quarters in a Freeport apartment building.

Construction continued. In September 1962, the completed baptistery was dedicated. The floor incorporated 30 stones from various European churches and cathedrals where some members of Good Shepherd had been baptized. The design of the baptistry, like much of the other artistic embellishment of the church, was the work of Adrian Harriers, a Dutch ecclesiastical artist.

The year of 1963 marked the entrance of the United Lutheran Church, and good shepherd with it, into the Lutheran Church in America. For the parish too it was a year of expansion, as the congregation voted in August to purchase a house for the pastors at 330 Hudson Ave., adjacent to the church property. And in November of that year, the spire with its surmounting cross was finally hoisted into place and dedicated. It rises 90 feet above the intersection of Brookside and Centennial Avenues.

A final building project was completed in 1964. Already the facilities were inadequate for some church activities so a wing was added to the south side of the building, incorporating office space and a choir room. At the same time, the front steps were reconstructed to provide a more efficient and aesthetically pleasing entrance to the church. All these changes were designed by William Siveitsen, a parish member. "The three bells in the spire were dedicated in March, and the rectory in April.

The regular ringing of the newly-installed bells, along with other bells at the new building of the Roman Catholic Queen of the Most Holy Rosary Church a few blocks away, provoked a brief controversy in the neighborhood. One local resident circulated a petition asking for substantial cuts in the bell-ringing schedule. While both churches did reduce their use of the bells to some degree, the controversy eventually petered out.

A Decade of Maturity and Transition

After the excitements of beginnings and buildings, the Church of the Good Shepherd spent its third decade in a somewhat steadier mode. Baptized membership had peaked in 1964; by 1974 it was down by almost one-third. In part this reflected the end of the "baby boom" years, but it also was influenced by demographic changes in the parish.

Roosevelt, for decades an interracial community, in the 1970s became predominantly Black in population. Good Shepherd, also racially inclusive from its earliest years, also saw a rapid increase in the proportion of Blacks in its membership and its active leadership. These changes helped infuse a new sense of mission and a new spirit of discipleship into what otherwise might have been an unexciting period in the church's life.

Another development in Christian education in the 1980s was the increasing number of Good Shepherd youth who enrolled at Long Island Lutheran High School. The parish became a member of the school's sponsoring association. While the congregation never realized an early dream of operating its own elementary school, some parish children attended, at various times in its history, the schools sponsored by Epiphany Church, Hempstead; Grace Church, Malverne; Trinity Church, Hicksville; Our Savior Church, Bronx, and Nassau Lutheran School, Mineola. Lutheran colleges which drew some young people from the parish included Upsala in New Jersey, Wittenberg in Ohio, Augustana in Illinois, and Muhlenberg and Gettysburg in Pennsylvania.

Another form of education was supported by the church when the Roosevelt Head Start program began using Church facilities in 1986. Other programs for the general community hosted by Good Shepherd at various periods include Boy Scouts, Alcoholics Anonymous and various civic groups.

Radical Transition

On December 15, 1989, Pastor Trexler retires from Good Shepherd. On December 9, 1990 the Rev. Jerome D. Taylor is installed as the second Pastor of Good Shepherd at a 4 PM Eucharist, Celebration by Rev. James b. Christ, Dean of the Southwest Nassau Conference.

April 21, 1991 was the installation of the first female acolytes at Good Shepherd. Up until this point, girls were not allowed to serve as acolytes. Rev. Jerome D. Taylor instituted thechange and Danielle Ballard, Jasmine Boxley, Meghan Crawford, Natasha Lish, Jenae Philip, and Amiya Wade were installed.

During this time (1991), a heavy wave of white flight began to plague Good Shepherd. Today there are only four white families left at Good Shepherd. The church today is a Black Multi-Cultural congregation consisting of African Americans; Jamaicans; Haitians; Dominicans;

Panamanians; Trinidadians and Virgin Islanders. About one-half of the church population is new to the Lutheran Church They have come from the Baptism, Roman Catholic, Methodist, Presbyterian, Moravian, Episcopalian, and AME Zion churches and one family from the Jewish faith.

In 1992 we further improved our music with the use of Lead Me Guide Me hymnal! A Roman Catholic hymnal inspired by Black Catholics. This was the beginning of our becoming more inclusive, paving the way for liturgical enculturation.

January 17, 1993, Good Shepherd hosted the Commemoration of Dr. Martin Luther King, Jr. service. This was sponsored by the African American Lutheran Association. There were over 400 in attendance, the largest ever. This large number came to experience the high church liturgical tradition of Good Shepherd.

Symbols and Rituals That Are Cultural

One of the symbols that give a clear and incisive view of the ethos of Good Shepherd is our multi-cultural identity along with our understanding that we as Black people are included through out the Bible. We have a balanced attitude towards biblical scholarship especially pertaining to its influence of our biblical interpretation. We read and study weekly what the biblical scholars have to say concerning the Word of God and how that Word impacts our lives. During our study we approach biblical scholarship with a critical and questioning attitude. We don't always agree with what is being presented, but we do learn from the experience just the same. I think that the best way to get at this is to tell a story. I (Rev. Jerome D. Taylor, pastor of Good Shepherd) remember one particular discussion in my Confirmation class of 8th graders concerning the make up of the people in the Bible. They wanted to know whether Black people were in the Bible and if so what part did they play in the unfolding drama of the Gospel and why aren't they mentioned. Normative biblical scholarship didn't give the answers we wanted but it did inform us that they were wrong in their lack of presentation of people of color in the Bible. We then moved from there to the area of Black biblical scholarship and found some fascinating answers. We discovered that the people in the Bible were not all White Europeans but instead people of color. My students were upset at biblical scholarship's portrayal and lack of portrayal of the people of color in the Bible. We continued with an intensive study of biblical history by first investigating what really happened during the

Renaissance Era. What we discovered during this time of so called rebirth, revitalization and reawakening was a systematic removal of the Black presence in the Bible. While the world was busy reinventing itself, the Church jumped on the ban wagon and said here's our chance to change things. The Church by the order of Pope Julius II, in 1505 then commissioned artist such as Michelangelo and others to recreate the people of color in the Bible into White Florentine Italian looking people. They changed all the crucifixes, icons, Madonnas, painting and all of artifacts that were originally done in the image of Africans. Some countries such as Spain and Poland kept to the original images of the people of the Bible as Africans. America continued to perpetuate this lie by portraying the people in the Bible a White in the movie industry. Even the White missionaries are teaching that the Africans' black pigmentation was the result of Ham being cursed by his father, Noah, and tuning black. When if fact there is nothing in the Bible that support that claim. In fact it was the opposite; the cursed ones were turned white. Naaman, Miriam, Uzziah and even the had of Moses turned white, not black. After this study my students felt better about themselves and our people all represented in the Bible from the beginning to the end. One of my students got expelled from her Lutheran school because she would not refute her learning that Black people were the original people in the Bible. I had to escort her with her parents to that school to meet with the principal and the two teachers who expelled her. We had a long discussion about biblical scholarship. I had the principal to make a phone call to the Lutheran seminary to talk with someone in the biblical department who confirmed my teaching as the truth. As a result, my student was reinstated in school and the two teachers had to offer a public apology to my student in front of the class. In essence, our multi-cultural identity and culture is a prominent symbol of who we are at Good Shepherd.

The membership of Good Shepherd over 60 years ago was typically a White/Caucasian congregation. Today she has a membership over 600 African American/Blacks baptized members with only 13 that are White/Caucasians. Of that number, 567 are baptized members, 362 are confirmed who commune, 32 unconfirmed.

Informal Decision Making

Informal decision-making takes place in many forms. It happens through: the Shepherd's Staff, a monthly newsletter of the congregation; it happens in the various ministry meetings; it happens through the Sunday bulletin; it happens through the Sunday morning announcements; it happens during the sharing of the Peace in the worship; it happens following the Mass during the coffee hour and as people leave the church; it happens once members get and then get on the phone and in many other ways. Sometimes important decisions are already made before the formal decision-making process takes place.

Financial Resources

The resources primarily come from the tithes and offerings of the congregation members. The tithes and offerings are based on what the annual budget is. For example, if the annual budget in voted on and approved by the Congregation Meeting and the amount is $250,000.00, then the congregation members will pledge to support that amount in order for the ministry of the church to be carried out. For the last seven years, the resources from the tithes and offerings have met or exceeded the budged amount. Other financial resources comes from: The Roosevelt Children's Academy makes a donation of $1,500.00 per month for the use of the undercroft for their school and they also pay one half of the church utilities; those who make contributions to the Memorial Fund, the Family Life Center Fund (building fund), the Helping Hands Fund (the pastor's discretionary fund used to help provide assistance to members and those in the community); T-Mobile Cell Tower, they pay the church $1,800.00 per month for the cell tower on church property and various fundraisers sponsored by different ministries during the year.

Our Vision Good Shepherd Lutheran Church is dedicated to improving the quality of life for members of our community as part of our Christian ministry. In carrying the church's mission, Pastor Taylor has a vision to build a community center that was identified as the result of a survey of community services provided by both local businesses and nonprofit agencies. The proposed Charles D. Trexler Family Life Center is unique in that it will not only address the documented community needs by providing Senior Day Care, and low cost banquet/meeting hall facilities, but it will, in the biblical sense, teach the community "to fish" by providing job training and employment opportunities, counseling, mentoring/tutorial programs, child care, dance studio, fitness center, and senior housing. Also recognizing that a long-term solution to addressing our community's needs lies in the planting of seeds that will foster perpetual growth and replenishing, the Charles D. Trexler Family Life Center will be the hub of a teaching congregation in which our spiritual leader, Pastor Jerome D. Taylor, will provide supervision and direction for third year theological students assigned by the Seminary to a congregation for ministry. Parish and intern housing will be available in the Charles D. Trexler Family Life Center, and partnering organizations and agencies will help to provide the network of support services offered to the community.

Women and children in poverty and senior citizens will derive the most direct benefit from this initiative, as their lives will be enriched through intergenerational activities, mentoring relationships, tutorial programs, housing, job training and employment opportunities in the computer and catering industries. The church community will benefit as a teaching congregation seeing its mission and vision in action through the partnership with Lutheran Social Services. The Roosevelt community, as a whole, will benefit from the provision of a center whose facilities offer a low cost banquet/meeting hall, as well as exercise rooms and childcare facilities. As such, the Charles D. Trexler Family Life Center will provide an infrastructure of human resources dedicated to the mission of overcoming the systemic causes of hunger and poverty in our community. We have already received a grant of $100,000.00 from the State of New York to help make this vision a reality.

A
History Of
Memorial Presbyterian Church
Roosevelt, New York

1920

1978

1990

INTERIOR

INTERIOR

Mission Statement As a community of faith devoted to Jesus Christ, Our Lord and Savior, Memorial Presbyterian Church will zealously promote the gospel of salvation, uphold economic, political and social justice for all while being responsive to the physical and spiritual needs of the community.

1857-1867	Valentine Smith distributes bibles for the American Bible Society in the hamlet called Greenwich Point (later renamed Roosevelt)
1867	Sunday School was held in the local school house with teachers and 30 pupils
	Portable organ purchased by Sunday for $150.00
	Chapel erected on land donated by Valentine Smith on Babylon Turnpike
	Bibles awarded for good attendance
1887	Sunday School Superintendent awarded scholars who brought in most new pupils.
1906	Gold watch presented for bringing most new pupils
1912	Award system switched to Cross and Crown system
1919	Thirteen women organized Willing Workers Society

1920	Church organized with help of Rev. Herbert Moyer and Rev Charles Park
1921	Committee appointed by Brooklyn Nassau Presbytery to organize church approved October
1922	Chapel housing Sunday school remodeled into a church
1923	Manse next to church built at cost of $12000
1924	Deacons established
1925	Land between original church and Frederick Ave was purchased
1928	$3,500 mortgage paid if full.
1929	Our Second Minister Dr. Steward and his wife die on the same day of heart attacks
1930	Christian endeavor established for young people
1935	Pipe Organ purchased by church
1952	Women's League formed by ladies and Rev Richard Owen
1967	Men's League organized
1970	Building Fund and project developed
1973	Rev Tuggle began his pastorship in September
1975	Building Fund intensified for second church
1976	Rev Tuggle and Marie Peoples wed November14, 1976
1977	Presbytery Synod approve building of second church-Ground broken and contract signed.
1978	New church building opened in Fall
1980	Man of the Decade Award goes to Rembert Brown
1980	Deacons Day originated
1980	Tree planted for Agnes Denton—member 61 years
1982	Pioneers Youth Program organized.
1982	Reach on Teach one tutorial program started
1984	Community wide Field Day was started for all local churches
1988	Young Adult Ministry organized
1990	New church opened
1990	Manhood Training started
	Christian Charm started
	Christian bible institute started.
1993	Rev. Tuggle 20th anniversary
1994	Purchase New Church Van
1994	Commercial Mortgage liquidated
1995	$200,000 grant for Youth Ministries awarded to Memorial Presbyterian Church Pathways Initiative Foundation

Calvary Baptist Church

Calvary Mission was founded in 1938 by the late Estrella Anderson and the late Mrs. Mary Johnson. The first services were held in the home of Mrs. Susie Goodwine.

The mission was later moved to the home of Mr. Clinton Dees on Brooks Avenue Roosevelt, NY. While at this location Calvary received eight new candidates for baptism, one of whom was our own J. Clifford Dennis. Service was again relocated to the Dennis' residence at 141 Underhill Ave Roosevelt NY.

Reverend Anderson shared, that God told her, "*to build a church that the footprints of time could not remove*". With this goal in mind Rev. Anderson and the faithful members of Calvary labored hard to accomplish this task. In 1939 a house was acquired and located on its present lot. On September 18, 1939 the church became officially incorporated under the Religious Corporation's Law, State of New York, as a Baptist Church, to be known as THE Calvary Baptist Church of Roosevelt NY.

Reverend Anderson and the membership worked hard and untiringly to enhance their place of worship to more adequately accommodate the needs of the ever-growing membership. Rev. Anderson sacrificing her salary and putting all moneys back into the church, made it possible for enumerable improvements to be made. Calvary was then able to acquire the adjoining property and the parsonage next door to the church in 1941. By renting the parsonage the income helped to defray some of the church expenses.

As of December 8, 1959, it was contracted that the lot, which the church stood officially, became the property of Calvary. The title was cleared and the property recorded on December 14, 1962.

By 1963, Calvary had been blessed sufficiently to break ground for our current edifice. The church cornerstone was laid and dedicated on May 17, 1964. Calvary's first journal was published that commemorate such a blessed occasion.

Every seed that is planted, when nurtured, flourishes, so is was with Calvary. However starting with only six members the divine order of the church as well as the membership grew rapidly as evidenced by its many editions namely, Rev. Rose Ferguson, associate minister and three evangelist, Sister Henrietta Haynes, Martha Smith and Lucille Tindal.

Church auxiliaries were organized in order to facilitate smoother Church operations. The Trustee Board; chaired William Warrick. The deacons board chaired bb Deacon William Warrick, the Deaconess Board Deaconess Leora Deassaure, the Senior and Junior Missionaries organized by sister Adelaide Jackson with sister Dorothy Sutton as president of the latter.

Reverend Anderson became ill and was unable to officiate after 1968; thus Calvary was without a pastor for five years. While visiting ministers provided religious service, Deacon Curry Green, Deaconess Leora Deassaure and other faithful members managed the church affairs.

As God has a master plan, He graced Calvary with a shepherd for it's flock when Rev. James L. Keel came to pastor in 1973. Transition is always difficult and Rev. Keel's appointed task was surely not an easy one; but God in His infinite wisdom and power never fails.

Under Pastor Keel's leadership Calvary Baptist has continued to grow. Reverend Keel gave up his fulltime employment and offered his full time service unsalaried until the church was financially sound. The membership has grown and the church has continued to develop both spiritually and structurally.

Many essential and significant changes have been made in organizing new auxiliaries and restructuring the overall format of previously established ones. The implementation of these changes was essential to facilitate operation in this ever growing society by advancing by with the times as well as meeting the mandates of church laws. Changes are generally met with confusion and resistance because all prefer the simplicity of sameness. Yes, times reflect the positive benefits of progressiveness in approach as you grow.

Added to existing auxiliaries was the formation of the Pastor's Aid club, Rev. Ronald Regular, president; Mission II, Sister Deloris Washington; Baptist Training Unit, Sister Edna Coakley; Floral Club Sister Mary McDaniel; The J.L. Keel Specials, originally coordinated by Sister Mae McClain, but the leadership later transferred to Cherelene Mc Clain and the Gospel Chorus with the now Rev. James Barber as the first president.

Under the Pastor's guidance with the help of faithful members, Calvary has made enumerable accomplishments. All structural changes have been done with minimal funds

The church has been completely renovated to more adequately meet the needs of the membership. We have been blessed with internal talents, which helped us accomplish a lot with very little Deacon Lee Baldwin along with the Youth of Calvary made some essential changes on the lower level of our edifice. As we progressed we were able to completely renovate the church, by adding a new pastorial office with sundeck extending from the office. Fortunately for us Mr. Johnson and his son did a beautiful job with these renovations. Revising the heating system was a major task but because Deacon Irving Mc Knight has expertise in this area even this was accomplished economically.

Other significant changes included, remodeling the kitchen and adding new appliances The exterior was repainted. The interior was repainted, repanelled, rewired and carpet installed. Mr. Polk converted our windows into beautiful stain glass windows. A piano and organ were also purchased. Additionally our own brother Willie Singleton made a replica of the crucifix that adorns our pulpit. Members have made countless contributions including the tithe box, tables, chairs, etc. God has said, "that we must be baptized both of the water, as well as the spirit". And so that we may fulfill His word we made our most significant improvement with the installation of our Baptismal pool, with overhead dawn. Brother Bagowitz chaired the fund raiser to help accomplish this task. Additionally the parsonage has been renovated

Pastor Keel's biblical teachings with the anointing of God has touched all of our lives We have been further blessed in that God saw fit to choose within the membership three workmen in His vineyard; Rev. James Barber, Rev. Simeone Forbes and Rev. Ronald Regular.

Our church from its inception, has had four mothers—the late Lester Saxton, the late Julia Williams, the late Willa Silva and the late Susie Bronson whom God has graced to witness 112 years.

Every church has a beginning a present and a future and each era plays a significant and essential role. Through it all one thing remains steadfast: No problem is insurmountable for we can accomplish all things through Christ who strengthens us.

We thank God for His many blessings and through his grace we hope to continue to build our church on a solid foundation with love understanding and spiritual growth.

Naomi Temple African Methodist Episcopal Zion Church

I must make this point before reflecting the history of Naomi Temple. During the 1920's a man by the name of Gerring started the KKK at the same address that Naomi Temple is presently located but I realized by analyzing my data that The Lutheran Church of the Good Shepherd was the one who sold Naomi Temple that property in 1962 before they moved to Brookside.

The AME Zion Mission was founded in May of 1962. The status as a mission was changed to an fully organized church in 1966. The founding of the church came about by the Rev. V. Lorna ST. Clair passing through the community of and finding this site available. He contacted the Presiding Elder of the Long Island District of the New York Conference, the Rev. J. W. Finley, who in turn contacted Bishop W.J. Walls, the then Presiding Bishop of first Episcopal District and other presiding ministers and elders of the conference. They negotiated to purchase this property at a cost of 58,000.

A survey of this community was made by various ministers of the conference. Some members of Rush Temple AME Zion Church of Jamaica, NY came and cleaned the church on Saturday May 12 1962. On Sunday May 13 the church school was held at 9:30 am with four children and four teachers.

The late Rev. Eldridge Gittens, Pastor of Rush Temple AME Zion Church preached the first sermon in June 1962. Rev. Gittens was in charge as pastor with the assistance of Brother Clarence Carr a local preacher from Rush Temple who in time gave up his gainful employment in order to be present with the members every Sunday morning. This arrangement continued and the membership grew.

The first move was the appointment of Trustees, comprised of two members held at the dedications October 1962 two more persons were added to the number, which made four active Trustees namely Mrs. Alberta Johnson, Chairman, Mrs. Marie Quarrels, Mr. Hever Brabham and Mr. Joe Ulmer

The Buds of Promise was organized and flourished under the leadership of Mrs. Barbara Carr The Stewardess board was organized with Mrs. Bernice Brabham as President. The first church choir was comprised of the church school children under the direction of Bobby Lawrence, a school student

At the Annual Conference in June 1963, the late Rev, Naomi Mims was appointed Pastor. Under the dynamic leadership of Rev Mims who was a singer as well as a preacher the church grew in membership and new organizations were formed.

Mrs. Willie Ziegler being the only member left in the Senior Choir became president of that Ministry. The trustees Aid was organized with Mrs. Nancy Morris as President.

In 1976 the Rutland Road property was purchased for 30,000.

In n1978 the Roosevelt AME Zion Church was named Naomi Temple AME Zion Church Incorporated after much consolation with the late Bishop Herbert Bell Shaw, Chairman of the Trustee Board, Mr. Richard Warren.

In 1975 Rev. Mims suffered her first illness which caused her to have to secure the help on Rev. Joseph Jones. Rev. Jones came as served as assistant Pastor for several years. Through his inspiration many young people joined the church and a Youth Choir was directed by him. He was instrumental along with the Gospel Chorus and some trustees in purchasing an organ. The building fund was established June 1978. The late brother Albert Ziegler was appointed Chairman.

In the earlier part of 1979 the late Pastor Mims became incapable of performing her full duties. The Rev. Rufus Daniels of Faith Baptist in Hempstead and the Rev. Dr. Eugene Purvis were called upon.

Rev. Mims requested that Rev. Purvis come and assume the duties of the pastor during the illness. He served for more than a year. He came with the true love and dedication of a brother in Christ. After the Pastor's death he was appointed pastor in June 1980.

Rev. Purvis reorganizes the church and geared it toward a broader and greater future, being very much aware of the role God with have the church play in our community. He launched a campaign to beautiful the edifice and to build a new one to accommodate the needs of the community as well as the church family.

Rev. Purvis was reappointed yearly until June 1993. Under his leadership, the physical church underwent renovations. The porch was enclosed with brick, new windows installed and a stairwell leading to the lower level was erected. Sometime later the Cornerstone Dedication Service was held. Two cornerstones were placed on each side of the steps. The Rev. Seth Martin Moulton was appointed to our parish in June 1993. His wife is Mrs. Rose Baker Moulton and their daughter Yude were welcomed with opened arms. Under Rev Moulton the Christian Education Department was revitalized. Mrs. Linda Settles-Brown served as director from 1994-98. Rev. Linda B. Vanager served as Director from1998-present. The Steward Board Chairmen have been Bro. Elmer Bryant (1993-99) and Bro Harry D Vanager (1999-present) Bro. Woody Allman continues to serve as Chairman of the Trustees The Senior Choir was disbanned and The Praise Ensemble and Youth Choir and the instruments of Praise were formed. The Gospel Chorus is still active. Present musicians are Sis. Betty Geralds, Sis. Kathy Oden and Dominique Geralds on the percussion.

The presidents of WH&OMS have been Mrs. Murtha Petty, Rev. Linda B. Vanager and Mrs. Katherine Bryant who served for many years and is the current president. Mrs. Florent Harleston continues to serve as Home Mission President. Since 1994 Vacation Bible School has been held in the evening from 6pm-9pm. It is scheduled for one week, Monday through Friday with closing worship on Sunday It is such a blessing to see the children as well as the adults worshipping, studying, dining, and praising God together.

In Febrary 1996 the Building Fund then called the Seed Faith Partnership held its first Annual Banquet. The RT Rev George W.C. Walker Sr., presiding Prelate of the North Eastern Episcopal District was the keynote speaker. The building fund was renamed "Project 2000". A cruise to the Caribbean was our fund raiser project and more than thirty members, families and friends spent the week from August 8-15, 1999, vacationing.

In September, 2001, Rev. Moulton gave up the pastorate of Naomi Temple to assume the position of the Presiding Elder of the Kansas City District as well as Pastor of the Kyles AME Zion Church in Des Moines, Iowa.

During the month of August and until the appointment of our new Pastor, the Rev. Isidoa Branch Sr., the newly appointed Presiding Elder of Long Island supplied our church.

At the Leadership Training Institute held at Desmond Inn, Albany NY, Bishop Walker appointed the Rev. Andrew Branch as pastor of Naomi Temple A M E Zion on Friday September 28, 2001. Pastor Branch preached his first sermon on Sunday September 30, 2001.

The Rev. Branch was reappointed in June 2002 to serve as pastor for 2003-2004 conference year.

Portions of the history of Naomi Temple AME Zion Church especially the period between 1981 through 1985 were not documented for lack of and historian. However, it is said that before the property was purchased from the Lutheran Church, Ku Klux Klan meetings were held in the basement of the church. Interesting . . . . Since we are called the "Freedom Church"

Project 2000 is progressing and the members are anxiously awaiting the ground breaking ceremony to take place in the near future; by the grace of GOD.

Mrs. Diane Warren still serves as our Sunday school Superintendent. Mrs. Willie Ziegler is now the Rev. Willie E. Ziegler Belt, an Elder and Mr. Richard Warren is now Rev. Richard Warren, a Deacon. The Rev. Dr. Eugene H. Purvis is pastor of Shaw Temple AME Zion Church, Amityville, NY. The Rev Clarence Carr is now the Rt. Rev. Clarence Carr, Bishop of Western Episcopal District. "ALL PRAISES BE TO GOD".

Updates:

- The Ministerial staff has increased there are now two Local preachers: Bro Harry D. Vanager, Sis Lavern White Bro. Billy Jones two Deacons Rev. Linda B Vanager, Rev. Debra Garrick, one Local Elder, Rev Richard P warren one Elder Rev. Willie E Ziegler-belt
- Rev. Linda B Vanager resigned as the Director of Christian Education at the end of 2005-2006 conference year. Sis Lavern is current Education Director.
- Sis Mary Gaskin served as the WH&OMS parent Body President, the current president is Dorothy McGuire.
- The Asst. Superintendent of Sunday school is Sis Gracie Settles
- We have additional worship services at 7:30 am
- We begin a 3rd Wednesday Re-Charge Worship Service Conference year 2006-2007

Disclaimers

The above information was obtained through interview and request by the writer for documents such as Church History. It is the writer's understanding that permission was granted through each pastor directly or indirectly.

It was my goal to have this project done sooner but many pitfalls including my own illnesses preempted completion in entirety.

At the beginning credited my father for his contributions. It is therefore only fitting that I start this section by recognizing his companion Mrs. Ernestine Parrish.

For the first twenty years or so of my life, my mother was a housewife, strong disciplinarian (for me and my rock head brothers) and sometimes a part-time worker. Many wonder how such a sweet, not so tall lady kept three bruisers in line. A quote comes to mind immediately "I don't care how big you get, I will get up on a stool, with a broom and beat your butt". Worked for me.

But I would like to thank them both publicly for being the most supportive parents you will ever see. Sometimes as many as three games in the same day, they never missed a game through high school and made most of my home games in college. There was one time where my youngest brother had to be at a weigh-in here at 8am and my parents made my 1:30 game at Colgate, in central NY, 40 miles south of Syracuse.

In 1978 my mom moved in at the main office at Roosevelt High School. I am told, she has always maintained a high level of professionalism and a co-worker once said "Mrs. Parrish you don't care who we talk about, you have nothing to say."

My mom would always say, "It takes six months to mind my business and another six to leave yours alone." She also sustains herself through a strong relationship with God. Her popularity, basically developed by just helping people with viable solutions to their problems in the main office, has led to people screaming her name in places as far away as South of the Border.

"Mrs. P" worked for a revolving door of Administrators with Mr. James Watkins departing as she arrived. We concur though, that the "Dream Team" of Administrators were Mr. Thomas Neary, Ms. Luella Cohn, Dr. Robert Nelson, Mr. Harvey Palmore, Mr. Durrell Blank and Marion Fleming. My mother will always hold her relationship with Mrs. Fleming in high regard. The Captain of the ship was my personal favorite. Dr. Phil Smith.

Mrs. P witnessed many oddities while in the "Main Office" as well. For example, seeing Administrators lose their job only to regain it at some later date. Once there was a Co-Principalship. There was also a situation when a Principal was hired with no secretary assigned to him. Usual Abnormalities that become commonplace in our schools.

Sports and Band

Roosevelt Football

I WAS FORCED to be more autobiographical in this section. This chapter looks at a lot of the students who attended Roosevelt from the sixties and on. Roosevelt did not have a high school until 1964 so all of the student/athletes had to choose one of the local high schools to attend. The John Mackey incident led to a high school being built. Len Meckeleavage was the first football coach and he coached until the 1973 season. He made national history from 1966-68 when he was undefeated three years with one season being untied, unscored upon. In speaking with Dr. Robert "Suave Bob" Tucker, my high school coach as well as a member of the first Roosevelt Football team in 1962, he says that "Coach Meckeleavage was excellent, He had come from Amityville High School, a dominant, class program, at that time was excellent at sideline diagnosis, he adjusted well to situations during a game. He had come from Amityville a dominant, class program, at that time.

Furthermore, it was said that coach benefited from the "white flight" as it brought in more talented black players. Some have also said that the best team is made of a blend of big strong white lineman and very quick black agilities players. Coach Tucker says that the first team was JV and they were undefeated and gave up only twelve points. The second year ('63) they lost 2 games. He names Earl Squires, Abe Perkins, Ronald Griffin, Bob Allan (a quick Jewish fellow) and Thaddeus Morris as top players of the time. He reflects on his brothers' careers Stanley and Ivy. Then upon graduation Coach Tucker moved on to Hampton Institute only to return and watch the greatness of the next few years while also playing for the Semi-pro Long Island Chiefs. I don't know personally but the football coach and the track coach John Mullen must have been real good friends because the same names appeared on both rosters. Good track people make good receivers and return people. Earl Squires and Ed Watson, Coach Tucker says, "Ran sub 10.00 seconds flat 100's way back in the "sixties". All-American Michael Stevens was a record holder in the broad, triple jumps, 220 and the relays. Galvaster Baber was the best in the county at his events as well. Being a former coach myself, I would be in good shape if I always had a deep threat on the field. As a matter of fact I did have one named Corey Mickens.

I played for Coach Tucker first in grade 9, my first year of organized football. I had always been too heavy to make the PAL teams. After a couple losing seasons "Coach Meckeleavage" left, a little frustrated after coaching nationally ranked teams. Coach Tucker took the Head position my junior year. In my senior year, co-captains; Charles Mahoney and I led the guys off the hill and into a championship. Winning was a benefit that went along with developing a comradery in life long friend Stephen Smith. We received co-championship jackets and we tied with Carle Place that year before the inception of the playoffs system. Don't seem to see that in the record books though. (Speechless).

After receiving the National Bank of North America for Outstanding Player Award, two years in a row, and winning the All-County/Gridiron 44 Award as well as some Professional tutelage from our line coach, Harvey" When I was down at Morgan" Palmore, Steve and I took off for Colgate University. We were recruited from Roosevelt to Colgate by one of the most remarkable Alumni players, Alvin Pearman an All-American in football and track. Alvin Pearman, returned to coach at Roosevelt before going on to Colgate University. When last I looked, he still held records in track He wound up being like a brother to me before his departure to Princeton University. He went beyond the call of duty coach and I think the greatest tribute would be a public, Thank you.

Good blood, breeds good blood, as they say, so if you happen to hear about some other great player named Pearman on the professional level (Jaguars) and another on the college level (Virginia Tech) they are his sons.

If I may detract from the Roosevelt story briefly, playing football created some different sorts of circumstances at times. I have to say that going to Colgate although a very prestigious and academically rich institution was still a shot of reality. The first issue was that I didn't realize how much different it would be playing on basically all black team in high school to basically an all white team in college. At the end of this project you will find a picture of my team at Colgate. It seemed to pretty much be an unwritten rule one brother on offense, one brother on defense and one brother on the bench. This is my opinion of course.

I can remember in high school playing against this guy that was on a rival Long Island powerhouse team, the Hempstead Tigers. His name was Bob Crowley. He played quarterback, and that Saturday we played against him he put a hurting on us. I was astounded when I found out he was leaving Morgan State for Colgate.

He had a great camp and was arguably the fastest if not the second fastest guy on the team, but of course he was moved to Safety. Something was wrong with us back then, "Blacks weren't smart enough to be a quarterback". I guess they fixed the mold because now we win Super Bowls and even run countries.

The next story I find amusing. When I was in high school we played this team called East Rockaway. I think it is safe to say they were in a down year. We had just been killed all week by our coach for losing to guess; Hempstead after going to their game the week before, against coaches wishes, and then lost to them after talking stuff from the stands. We were so tired of running etc, and beating on each other all week when we got to East Rockaway it was all over.

Then you could swing a forearm (illegal now). I was using that technique all game and by third quarter the guy over me was bleeding from the nose. I have to admit he gave up a number of pounds to me but he was tough as nails. I would like to meet him. After beating on this guy for 3 quarters a teammate, after coming off a safety blitz, says to me in the huddle, did you see what I did to his face? I was speechless. Fast forward to spring 2009; I received a copy of the new Colgate Scene, a magazine which used to be a boring newspaper. Now it has flair and pizzazz!! I was curious and opened it up to find a section called "Ask Raider", a "sports trivia" section. The question was something like; What former Colgate football player broke All-Pro Former NFL player, Howie Long's ribs in a game? Again I was speechless. I remembered the game well so this was what I emailed the editor:

Firstly I would like to congratulate you on the New Scene, Cudos.

But . . . . I was going to overlook something written in Ask Raider but then I realized a conflicting version of the story lies between the covers of my book project "One Square Mile" to be released this summer. Here are some little known facts about that Villanova game

1. Dan Mastrella was a Defensive tackle and was not even on the field when Howie Long was on the field. He was platooned on offense as an experiment.

2. Offensive Line Coach Dave Barton came to all the offensive linemen and said our center had a bad headache from Howie's teammate Mattasavage the other defensive tackle and he asked us to help out whenever possible. (Mattasavage was actually the guy I didn't want to deal with. He was a beast.)
3. The Colgate offense at that time was run by Chris Palmer and we ran the Delaware Wing-T which I in turn ran as a high school coach.
4. In this offense there is a lot of blocking down, fold blocks, kick outs etc. but not much straight man on blocking.
5. The play believed to have hurt HL was a 37 kick out which calls for the center to block backside tackle and then up on backer. The left tackle blocks down (ribs) on the playside d tackle (HL). Playside guard kicks out the end.
6. On this play, that day Angelo Colisimo had a sixty-seven yard run.
7. The person who was the source of the trivia was on the sideline at the time rooting the offensive line and called out my name a few times so I don't know how his memory could be so scrambled.
8. Who was the blocking tackle, me Sheldon Parrish Class 81'. Playing next to me was Kevin (Kelly) Green, who was very helpful in the trenches.

I commend Colgate for finally realizing that it needs an effective Diversity Professional. When I played only three African-American players were on the team. One on the D, One on the O and one on the Bench. And one of the best quarterbacks to ever hit that field was Robert Crowley 80' who was a transfer from Morgan State. But back then we weren't smart enough to play QB LOL. I played against Rob in High School so I know how good he was. But look now we QB, we Coach and win Super Bowls even become President. Holy Cow. Colgate missed a lot of excitement in those days. Thanks.

Sheldon

I would be remiss in stating that this situation was not at all indicative of Dan Mastrella, he was one of the strongest dudes on the team and a cool guy as well.

Sorry to reach so far but while I am out there I would like to mention that when I first came back to town I was job hunting and obtained an interview with then Grumman Aerospace. I was sort of nervous that day and I was going over my answers in my head. I had to wait awhile and I remember some how it had circulated that I was a football player. I was shown down a hall to this office and when I walked in former New York Giant Harry Carson was sitting at the desk. He stood up and shook my hand and everything I was trying to remember to say went in a trash. Needless to say I didn't get that job. Although I respect his career maybe being a avid Dallas Cowboy fan killed it for me. I lived in Dallas, Texas for a year and my first father in law, Mr. Hendricks had a family member in the NFL front office and I sat at the fifty yard line, 2 rows up on the visitors side for the whole season. At one of the games I attended, at halftime they honored the State of Texas Hall of Famers. I leaned over and had the opportunity to talk with Tony Dorsett and Earl Campbell.

Anyway, Let me bring it back home. Back in the days "The Ice Cream Parlor" next to Franklin National Bank used to be a hang out place and sometimes Vie Brock's in Freeport after the game. Many a great play became celebration material in these two venues. Our memories also reflected the short life of Clayton Heath who was another great Rider who went on to play for the Colts and the Dolphins and let us not forget Wally Perkins and Allan Parrish. Some other names to mention that were synonymous with track and football were Russell Brown, Ken Mazyck, Leon Glass, Gordon Glass, Ed Kennedy and Anthony Gilbert. It has been a long time since we have had players ranked on the level of these individuals although we have had some to make it to the NFL.

Until recent years there has not been much consistency in track. It was a great loss when track coach extraordinaire, Charles Gilreath left for greener pastures in Freeport. Football Coach Joe Vito presently coaches the track team also and he has been credited with making the team respectable.

Coach Tucker was a biology teacher and also. Our first season we went 4-4 and the second season we tied for a championship at 6-2. This was before the playoff system began. Coach was around one more season then he moved on to Uniondale School District and a successful Administrative career. In 1980 Ken Mazyck, Don Crummell and myself all worked under the new head coach Victor Gaffan. The three of us had something else in common and Jerone Pettus(Wisconsin); we all played for Coach Meckeleavage.

This coaching staff had 1 Thorpe Award Winner (Best Offensive player in Nassau County) in Robert Lee (AIC-Springfield Mass). Coach Gaffan then moved on to Uniondale as well.

The next head coach was Don Crummell and Ken Mazyck and I were his assistants. We were blessed to have some real fine players in Terence Wisdom who signed a letter of intent to Syracuse as did Edward Hobson and Elliott Fortune signed with Georgia Tech. Both Terence and Elliott had short NFL careers. Elliott is also remembered for the night he was captured by ESPN when he became the first high school to break a backboard during a basketball game. Another great player Kenny Squires went on to University of Maine.

I succeeded Don Crummell as the next head Football Coach in 1989. A very good friend and colleague Leon knight was my assistant. William Mingo (Delaware State) was the quarterback and a defensive back and still holds the record in Nassau for a 98 yard fumble return. I have to recognize Andrew Pittman who was one of the toughest kids I know. He and Ira Toliver made the Varsity team as 8th graders only because we refused allow them to play as a 7th grader. So Andrew played Varsity Soccer that year. He had one game in his career where he scored five touchdowns.

Coach Joe Vito was my successor and is the present coach. His longevity has brought a host of awards, accolades and Championships to both players and to himself. He coached James Wyche (Syracuse) now a member of the Jaguars (NFL) as well.

Coaches Corner

ALTHOUGH MANY THOUSANDS of people have been in attendance at Roosevelt Rough Rider football games many did not know of an institution that existed and was present at every game, but the coaches did. During games, right by the hill, along the Softball field backstop was assembled an ideology. You always saw the Guru's perched as we looked over our right shoulder, ready to critique our every play. Of course most waited to see the success or lack there of before they second guessed our play calling, but the more astute knew what we should have called, as a play, before we called it. Tough as it was, we still felt the love. We meorialize some and honor others now as most of you have transitioned from this life. You may come across these names at other times in this project but I make mention of Jim Brown, Frank Brown, Jim Simpson, Elmer Bryant Sr., Luther Johnson, Marion Gary, Univester Smith, Oscar Glass and then Charles Dudley and George Jones who still manage to mentor. Never forget Mr. Jenkins, Mr. Dean and Mr. Amar. We thank you for the tough love and support.

Baseball, Soccer, Volleyball, Bowling and Wrestling have all had individual stars but not great "championship" teams.

Baseball has had some good teams that never seemed to materialize into powers but I must mention an historical event. A player by the name of Rod Harris pitched the first baseball no hitter in 25 years of baseball history at Roosevelt. A 3-1 victory over Seaford, striking out eleven and walking three batters.

Roosevelt High School Basketball

The first coach was Ray Wilson who stayed on only a few seasons as he was Julius Erving's coach and he departed to the University of Massachusetts and was with the Hall of Famer during the balance of his career. My next entry says that Charles McIlwain was the second coach, Curt Fisher the third, Harvey Palmore the fourth, Morris Brandon the fifth and Heyward Hammond followed him. It is safe to say that all these gentlemen secured a place in Roosevelt's history in other ways besides just being a coach. Mr. MacIlwain was the first African-American teacher in the district. After many years as the Assistant principal at Roosevelt High School he became the principal at Centennial Avenue.

Curt Fisher, while working in the district had the reputation for dealing with the more challenging learners. He then parlayed his great patience into a great political career. Harvey Palmore's team became well-known for their great team defense culminating with a Long Island Championship, Southeast Regional Championship and a trip to the state tournament in Great Falls NY in 1978. Some popular names during that run were George Holt, Lance Jenkins, Lawrence Leach, Jeff Stevenson, Mike Miller, Terence Parrish, Jeremiah Everett, Curtis Hammond, Gordon Douglas, Carl Baldwin and Anthony Fitchett.

Harvey Palmore filled the vacancy of Athletic Director created by the departure of long time AD Arthur Flechner. A position he would hold twice at Roosevelt. Up until this time Roosevelt basketball was a fast paced game. Mr. Palmore named his successor Morris Brandon; a disciple of Bobby Knight and the half-court offense. Fresh from college, I was present in the stands to hear all the disapproval of this new style of basketball. Especially, in the beginning when Brandon had to clear house so that the ideology of the team would reflect his. This style of play, after a slow start soon coveted many championships. This era's ballplayers included Charlie Bryant, Mike Hammond, Rodney Heath, Todd Parrish, Melvin Fitchett, Anthony Brown, Barry Abercrombie, Kevin Calhoun, Dennis Barmore, Damon Sessions, Todd Hardy, Brian and Paul Chin.

Sadly we lost this great motivator, mentor, educator, coach and friend in October 1990. His long-time assistant Tommy Hammond replaced him that season and won the County Championship "on a shot at the buzzer". The opposing coach (Arnie Sims) commented that he "had been beaten by a ghost". Coach Hammond won "Coach of the Year" (07).

Girls Basketball

There have only been three coaches for Girls Varsity Basketball Miss Attridge was the first coach for Girls Varsity Basketball. Rick Brown is credited with the creation and the fundamental stages of the program and Don Crummell has been credited with taking it to the next level with County Championships and an appearance in the state tournament as well. The accolades read as follows:

NEW YORK STATE RUNNER UP—1994
LONG ISLAND CHAMPIONSHIP—1994
NASSAU COUNTY CHAMPIONSHIP—1988, 1989, 1994
DIVISION CHAMPIONSHIP—1988, 1989, 1993, 1994, 2001, 2002
NEWSDAY COACH OF THE YEAR—1983
NASSAU COUNTY COACH OF THE YEAR—1989, 1993, 2001, 2007
WOMEN'S SPORTS FOUNDATION COACH OF THE YEAR—2002
PLAYER'S AWARDS   ALL DIVISION 30   ALL CONFERENCE 25
ALL COUNTY 26   ALL LONG ISLAND 6

Some players who helped make girls program grow over the years are. Kim Jackson, Latasha Thomas, Monica Morgan, Tiera Mayrant, Bess Simpson, The Archibald sisters, Neisha Ferguson, Seretta McKnight, Faith Colter and Angie Lucas. There is a whole host of players that have given their best for the Gold and Blue, far too many for me to name them all.

Cheerleaders

I admit that as an athlete and as a coach I have realized the value of cheerleaders. There is no better support entity at a game but it is quite hard to separate them into individual greatness, I know that Barbara Floyd was a popular name in the sixties as a cheerleader and then as a coach in the seventies. I also remember the passing of another popular cheerleader and town favorite Sheila Griffin who transitioned while we were school age. That was the first funeral I ever went to. I picked a very sad one for my first.

I know that because of devotion to team spirit and allegiance to the good ole' Blue and Gold"; many girls started as early as eight years old, cheered through PAL and then on to the high school, only to return back to PAL to coach. The history at this time must acknowledge, Barbara Floyd, Janet Coles, Brooksie Hunt and Monique Gooding-Hamasham for long tenure and service to make the cheering squad tops on the island annually.

The Roosevelt High School Band

I know that presently Mr. Blank is probably upset that all his long and tedious work is going to waste. It has been over five years since the band has taken the field at Hofstra University for the Newsday Marching Band Festival, a competition that Roosevelt was always superior. We have gone away from the understanding that extra-curricular activities such as band, orchestra, chorus and sports as well as a great vocational alternative breeds student interests and perseverance. My niece is now a student at Uniondale High School, Uniondale NY. My mother went to a music program there that was just short of ultimate greatness. The choir was scheduled to participate in the McDonald's Gospelfest two days later. That must inspire a few kids to stay in school. It is the total experience in school that makes the student more marketable. Colleges have to deal with large numbers so they look to see which potential choices will have great value in the quality of campus life

In Roosevelt band suffers more than sports only because of less popularity. In my day everybody played an instrument or sang and belonged to one band or another. Two years ago I had the opportunity to see unkept uniforms and instruments that kids have used since the "sixties". The music department is a forgotten concept down in the forgotten wing. Parents this is why you most vote for your budget you hurt a lot of kids on Austerity.

Roosevelt Park

I moved to Roosevelt shortly after the completion of Roosevelt Park. The park might have actually been the reason for "White flight" in the surrounding area but I have since learned that there were deeper issues. Stereotypically thinking, a basketball court can have an affect on a neighborhood. That park was not built for my family. They did put the right director in charge though and "The legend" of Nancy Washington still lives in that park long after moving on. Mrs. Vailles-White, has also managed to hold it down at Roosevelt Park (now Rev Arthur Mackey Sr. Park) and has already received accolades to that affect.

In the early days the baseball field had a grass infield that was well maintained. There has always been a scenic path leading to the rear of the park approaching the picnic areas. A stream used to run beside the path into the lake in the park The lake would be stocked annually for fisherman. In the winter, there was always a sign on the gate letting you know whether there was ice skating that day. They would drive a county truck out on the ice and test the safety level. But why does it look completely different from Centennial Park?

When Roosevelt Park was built the planners envisioned whites still holding down the North side of Washington Avenue. The park they were intending non-whites to use was "of course" built on Babylon Turnpike. No grass, a few trees, something resembling a park in the five boroughs.

Another sidebar before getting back on task. The particular location of the Cerebral Palsy (1952) is one to ponder. I took the National Teachers' Exam in 1988. I remember that the key to me passing all three parts in one shot was that I focused on the year of the handicapped. I remembered that all sidewalks, by-law had to be broken at the corner so that they would be wheelchair accessible and that all parking lots had to fall in line as well. I also remember the length of time for the curbs to be broken on the path between the Cerebral Palsy Center and the front gate of Roosevelt Park. This, of course forced workers to push the wheel chairs in the street for years.

Having a handicapped family member I remember the cruelness of society that labeled these individuals "cripples" etc. instead of "physically challenged". The Cerebral Palsy is a campus now. They probably hire more "Roosevelt" people than the school district does now, but before all the successful telethons, they were a one building operation. Why that location?

Right on the dividing line between the races. On the black side! Somehow were blacks and "cripples" in the same category? One thing visitors and workers were assured of was a quick easy way out of town. I have heard from some of the employees who say they have never actually been "in Roosevelt" (Over the Meadowbrook and out).

As I get back on task, I must reflect back to the formative years, having to get my chores done on Saturday so I could get across the street to the courts early because I wanted to have enough time to play before the big boys came and took the courts from us. I have learned that this behavior goes on in every park but the difference at Roosevelt was that at 1:00 pm on a Saturday a game might include Julius Erving, George "Tree" Green, Ollie Taylor, Lavern Tart and others, who were of ABA (Nets) caliber. As a youth watching to see the result of the greatest "shot blocker" in the area, in George Green trying to stop one of the greatest offensive players of all time in Dr. J. was more than just simple entertainment. Free too!! All you had to do was wait for that brown paneled station wagon to descend into the park. I am going to mention some other last names of ballers like the Saunders boys, Creech, Jones and the Burgess Boys. Most people don't even realize that the first tournaments took place in Roosevelt Park, sometimes during the "Teen Canteen". Picture sitting on the hill, with your beverage of choice watching the game, listening to some funk, on a hot summer night. Free. It didn't get any better than that.

During the late sixties and early seventies Monday and Thursday nights were popular during the summer, at Roosevelt Park. Being the oldest, I was the son charged with maintaining the lawn at our house. On Tuesday and Friday mornings I had to search the lawn for empty bottles and refuse that would damage the lawn mower. The night before, the park had transformed itself into a large outdoor concert. At that time, instead of the residents of the county going to Eisenhower Park, each local county park had its own concerts. The concert mobile would come to the park (summer jobs) and then they would lock the gates so cars could not enter. Then a couple of bands would play for the night. People would come from all over Long Island to sit in the grass or stand and watch the groups with sessions going from 7 until about 10pm. This was the "Teen Canteen".

By the time the eighties came upon us night concerts had been a thing of the past due to cutbacks and security concerns but weekend happenings picked up. Sundays especially were "hot" because the basketball court would be packed and where there are ball players there are girls to watch them play.

Sundays became so hot that there would be times when my brothers and I were on vacation, but we made it back by 4pm or soon after. The days of youth brought the roller skating mobile twice a week, the arts and crafts lady, puppet shows, Archery, Punt, Pass and Kick, Santa and the Easter Bunny. With at least five camps rotating use at the park I know these services could be used.

Centennial Park

Nassau County built two parks in Roosevelt during the sixties. I truly believe that if the county new the real affects of the "white flight" they would not have built these parks so close together. If you check the addresses of Nassau County Parks you will see that most are towns apart. Centennial Park was built strategically to reflect it's intended users. Anything built on Babylon Turnpike was for blacks.

Sidebar again; before "restoration" I wondered how Ulysses Byas (formerly Theodore Roosevelt school) was in such disrepair while Centennial Ave School was used as the anchor school during renovations to all the other schools. They were built at the same time, from the same plans. Obviously the school on the Southside, in the "section" was not built with the same intent, such is the difference between Roosevelt and Centennial Park. Different users, different philosophy. And years later why did we name this school Ulysses Byas? (Oops!)

After hearing "Man-Law" that Julius Erving used to take quarters off the top of the backboard, after watching him named one of the fifty best players to ever play the game of basketball, that school should have been named after a local hero, not for a controversial former Superintendent. Maybe if he had raised the budget at least $1 per year; we wouldn't have had to rebuild his namesake. There would have been money in the budget to have maintenance on more than the grounds outside his office (oops!)

Julius patrolled the grounds in the "sixties". I have learned recently through our Alumni Website that a Principal who also, by the way was a mentor and friend of Julius, Dr. Earl Mosely should have been the name of the school.

During the eighties, things switched during the week. Roosevelt sort of became a "kiddie park" and Centennial had people lined up four rows deep outside the fence to watch the summer league tournament. Park Director, Mr. White, Frank Stalling, and Wesley Malloy had a lot to do with the success of the tournament. At one point, they were able to lure Budweiser as a sponsor and the tournament brought out the most known and talented ball players on Long Island and NYC. The action was hot and heavy and was well attended because, "where there are ball players, there are girls". I had asked one of these gentlemen to submit something to me because I believed that they could realistically capture all the drama. They were all quite shy in this respect or maybe they felt the same way I did when I worked for the district. "Better keep my mouth shut on this one". But when I tell you all the big names that came to that tournament mostly present or former NBA players you would be amazed. All in "One Square Mile"

WRYC

Before the "White flight" Mansfield Avenue was part of the Jewish area in town. When I used to walk to Nassau Rd as a young man I would walk down this street because my favorite bus stop to Hempstead and the "Hoagie House" was located on the corner of Nassau Rd and Mansfield Avenue. The synagogue and attached building became the Roosevelt Youth Center. In the basement of this complex funding was granted to build a radio station run by the students. Brother Ujima, the Shockleys and Chuck D were very instrumental in the operation of this Radio station. Given what has followed they would then have to be regarded as trailblazers in the Hip-Hop music industry.

Canines

This was a special section dedicated to man's or sometimes woman's best friend.

When we were growing up in the neighborhood there were dogs that had reputations. There was a man who once lived on Astor Place at the corner of Lincoln, who had two Great Danes. Mr. Peachy, rumored a former NYPD officer, believed in training his dogs. Everyone used to curb their dog along the fence at Roosevelt Park and Mr. Peachey walked his dogs down Elmwood, my block.

One day I noticed that part of the training was to leave the dogs as far up the block as possible and make them sit. He would keep walking towards the park. And on a simple command they would gallop towards him.

I could never forget the feeling of coming out of my door headed for the street and finding myself directly in between Man and his best friends. At one point, he was reduced to one dog, for whatever reason, but the sight of an approaching excited stallion look a like was more than one's shorts could bare. Once we were walking from Theodore Roosevelt (UB) and as we passed the open gate where the dogs lived, former teammate and neighbor, Leo Carter yelled Oh S—the dogs. He was on the street side of the curb and he hopped this car with three steps and took off. I don't know which situation caused the most interest. The dogs or watching Leo do this car in three steps. Leo was also the one who called out "There's Mr. Dinky, while we once walked in the woods by the Cerebral Palsy Center. He has changed all that devilment now for a different calling.

Another feared dog was Cecil Riley's Germen Shepherd especially since Cecil had relocated. The dog lived on Beechwood Avenue and he bit me one morning. Good thing I had on a fake leather so the bite was not quite as penetrateable. I was on my way to school and he had jumped out what used to be the middle window in the front door. He had broke that out on a different occasion. Mrs. Riley, a very nice lady, who also taught in the school district came and got the dog brushed me off and gave me more paper to replace my notebook and sent me on to school. She gave me more paper because it had rained and during the skirmish I had dropped my notebook in the water.

Later on, I was given a Brindle American pit bull pup which I called "Crusher". Everything I owned then was named "Crusher". Probably me and my Dad's last Father and son project was building Crusher's house. It must have been pretty awesome because after Crusher passed on two little boys came by and asked if they could have the house.

I don't see many dogs in the neighborhood any more but the very last to maintain the perimeter was a real Brindle pit bull owned by the Hill family on Mirin Ave. Rio was his name. I had this habit of getting out of my car just as Rio would be passing through late at night usually between 2 and 4 am. Sometimes he would even stop to watch me walk in the house. Not a friendly glance of course, Rio was trying to figure out if he was going to have to bite me that night. Or maybe, just maybe he was trying to figure out where I was coming from. He always seemed to be coming from the same direction as well.

Roosevelt's Economic Forecast for the Future

D URING 2007 WE saw some interesting articles in Newsday that might not mean much by themselves but together they may very well spell the end of Roosevelt as we know it. Donald Trump won the rights to put a casino at the Jones Beach restaurant property. Furthermore, he has won the right to start with an underground level. In my opinion it will not be long before he controls the waterfront and legalized gambling will challenge the Shinnecock Reservation games very shortly. For those of you who don't know, the senior members of government had fought long and hard to keep the Long Beach and Jones Beach coastlines from gambling control. There has been gambling going on at the Reservation because the law sets aside the Shinnecock Reservation as a separate legal entity within the state causing the other residents of the state to be discriminated against.

To the North starting at Hempstead Turnpike, Wang and his group published plans to revitalize the whole Mitchell Field Complex. These plans have included renovating the Marriott and the Nassau Coliseum as well as extending a spur of the Long Island Railroad right into the complex, also to include a Semi-professional baseball team. Remember what the impact was on the development of Atlantic City. The environment around the billions in casinos was depressed and disadvantaged.

As taxes steadily increase in Long Island and in the Roosevelt area, roles have reversed. For so many years we looked for answers on how to build new schools. The fact that the building on Rose Ave was still being used after some 80 years or so was deplorable. Just on the other side of the new millennium, the consensus changed to building new schools even as the public conversation was about merger. I believe the plans are one in the same. When they draw the new map they will be able to offer the surrounding towns' residents the "golden opportunity". Oddly enough, one of my former white colleagues said that he had been actually looking for a house in Roosevelt (???) When you connect the dots with the fact that for many years the town tried to renovate the schools since he conditions had been such that cubicle dividers were setup to separate classes physically but were still distracting sound wise, during a time when Roosevelt enjoyed the existence of many positive and successful programs. Now, in a paradox of transition and transformation, there stands a pillar of education in its place. When has society ever built such an edifices in a black community without other intensions or the "big picture in mind". We have, for so long, been maligned by the stereotype that we would just destroy any such ideology.

But then a mild mannered—soft-voiced Superintendent came to town and made it all happen. He made the paradigm shift seem so viable. You see towers as monuments to students, whose numbers don't come close to maximum capacity to fill those classrooms. To be in need for so long and then to be given more than you needed always made me nervous. Such pillars of education were not built for our African-American children. Why has the NYS Department of Education taken so much heat in reference to Roosevelt's problems? Is it because somebody forgot to analyze the connection to the Socio-Economic ideologies which were so duly noted back in the "seventies" placing blame on political decisions. Who is responsible for the tax formula? The main complaint of the taxpayers is that their taxes are too high. When more business and commercial taxes are collected, residential taxes are reduced or not increased. Who is responsible for allowing business in town? Who is responsible for so much property laying dormant on Nassau Rd?

The building just finished in town looks marvelous. If I remember, the construction firm that built its original frame, was also supposed to complete that building and occupy it with offices. The firm was to occupy a floor in that building somewhere around 1988. At last look, it is still unoccupied. Where else in America would it take twenty years to build a building?

Again, at Colgate University they taught us to be analytical in our thinking. Hitherto a well respected gentleman Aaron Scott stated that he felt Roosevelt "has been in decline the last forty years". I concur. But Why? Having one time sat in an economics class or two (my major) if an instructor would have drawn up the present status of the town he would have sighted poor planning from the outset. But was it intentional?Hmmm . . . . ?

Moreover, if you analyze the need for the town to be able to afford its own school district, you would need to maximize the use of vacant lots on Nassau Rd. and convert to as much commercial property as necessary. If more business is needed to reduce residential taxes then, why does it appear that the owners of all said property are paid not to build? How else could you afford the property to be bare for so long? Furthermore, why hasn't there been a freeze on housing starts?

Sources say that bankers and realtors make easy for immigrants to buy houses in Roosevelt. We must ask ourselves who did the predominantly black school district residents pass a bond for. Themselves or the future residents?

Many African-Americans have had to walk off and leave their homes because of the balloon mortgage deals. At the end of the soft affordable years they could not afford the principal part of their loan.

Polling the community residents; I found that most, basically feel that twenty years from now Roosevelt's face will not have the same color. A lot of the seniors questioned believe that because of their age this will be someone else's problem. While some move, others try to hold on to what they have hoping that taxes won't eat them up. Since I have loved ones in town, I remain prayerful that their plans are successful. But the system has no feelings and policy makers have always agreed that the quickest way to move a mass of people is through taxation. Some detractors think it can't be done. People in power can do anything they want. Ask the Indians who originally inherited the land Roosevelt sits on.

Closer analysis of the surrounding area would yield the fight going on in Hempstead proper as their skyscape is threatened by the infiltration of high rise condominiums. The single-family household mentality is not inviting to the rich developers. The return on a corporate or condo multi-unit development will make the Hempstead part of this thoroughfare well worth the fight. Once the philosophy changes to "whatever I can build", you will find that African-Americans will be priced right out of the housing market. "Revitalization is one word that always scares me". As these new economic strategies merge towards each other housing prices as well as taxes will escalate to a point that will be unreachable by all people of color except maybe the Asians and Arabs. Is that why a prior school superintendent thought that Chinese would be a very important language to incorporate into the curriculum when the town has become approximately 40% Latino? In the next election period if we continue as a town to let certain elected officials remain silent and just take "photo ops" at community events to prove their worth then time just might have gotten away from us. The first thing we must do is try to eliminate all the ideologies that seek to divide us. We have diversity issues that must be cured from within. What a strong and powerful Roosevelt it would be if African-American and the Latinos were on the same page.

During the month of February I had the opportunity to watch the "Eye on the Prize" series. If you are not familiar, it is a series about the Civil Rights Movement. It appeared that even to the most vital intricacies, the people relied on and trusted the church. Every Socio-economic ill was essentially addressed by the church family. I was then reminded of something Walter Mackey Jr. said to me. He said "back in the "fifties" he said the banks and merchants in town were not to keen on issuing our people loans. So when your neighbor got into a small bind financially you would have his family over for dinner and the men got together, and then the church got together and the problem was soon resolved".

I have spoken with many local ministers and they maintained their anonymity, some of them actual former classmates, others I competed against during those athletic days. Many of them expressed their frustration with the idea that the clergy can't seem to get on the same page. They say "that the size of the church has more to do with the criteria then your desire to heal the problem". Some even go as far as to say that some of the clergy representing Roosevelt do not live or have a church in the town and have bullied the smaller churches into following their leadership, when it should be in reverse. How much division can One Square Mile take? It is a new day. I am told that when Arthur Mackey Sr. and clergy stepped into Town Hall people began to reschedule their appointments. It might be time to Galvanize.

Lets have a major multi-cultural parade and festival, Lets all participate in the Memorial Day Parade. Something that affects us all. How about building a Astroturf field where football and soccer programs can flourish, like other towns.

How quick we would find out that we are all the same. How quick we could galvanize to get the things that matter most to Roosevelt citizens. The empowered Roosevelt voting base. The biggest respect any of us can get. It will take a strong Roosevelt to battle the Trump's and the Wang's and others.

Two to three years from now you will see the "powers that be" start to enact new laws and administer old ones Through restriction of one family to single-family households and taxation people will be pressured to move to sell their homes to the original owners who will then be ready to take back the town they gave up forty years ago. A few weeks ago a man who said he worked for the Census department knocked at the door and he said he was sent out to remind residents to fill out the census truthfully "this year" because it was going to be real important???? Then he asks "Sir is this a single family home?" Why was that important? Most of all the residences in Roosevelt are single family so where did that come from?

Roosevelt, a town between Hempstead and Freeport with access to multiple highways and byways Prime Real estate. A town they let African-Americans borrow since 1960.

Roosevelt, Reasons to be Tearful Part I. (written and public dispersed (2007)

FIRST I THOUGHT to include this subject matter in my book but decided it needed separate attention as not to be confused with any sensationalism.

For those of you who traveled the road paved with "Gold and Blue" during the sixties and seventies then you would be saddened by all that has been lost since that era. I have been on record publicly about the demise of the Planetarium. For those of you unfamiliar with that theory it was a "state of the art system" geared at teaching students about the Solar System. It highlighted placement of planets and star clusters. The domed ceiling was an actual replica of the Solar System when the lights were lowered by the one qualified instructor, Mr. Todd Schelgel. The civil rights movement and the riot of 72" in Roosevelt had forced the district to search for the most qualified Black teachers and the most liberal minded White teachers and employ them. We can partly thank Emily Moore for that. During the late seventies and early eighties some of these professionals were heavily recruited by neighboring school districts Freeport, Hempstead and Uniondale. Roosevelt refused to come close to the salaries offered, so for most it was a "No Brainer" Mr. Schlegel, for family sake, chose to leave. But I was always taught that if you are prepared not to pay the top man then you better have a well trained second to take his place . . . .

It seems that after his departure that the room was allowed to be trashed and then that was the reason for not spending the money to fix the mistake. Now the room once a detention room is now a teacher's lounge with a domed ceiling.

Down one way to make education fun and easier for our children

Three doors down is the music room. I flash back to Ms. Davis, Dr. Swack, Mr. Blank and Mr. Turner a real tight music department. I remember when the chorus schedule and the band schedule were built into the school day and you alternated your lessons with your section. The trumpets would go around to the lobby of the auditorium to have their lessons. I imagine other instruments did as well. We had a orchestra, with real musicians who played the Tympani, Oboe and Bassoon really got to shine. The choir was equally drilled and proficient. Next door, the room that if caught being disruptive, you would see a side of a little man you didn't want to see. Mr. Blank was very devoted to what went on in that room, equally so, Mr. Turner. If you were to go in that room you would cry at the damaged old instruments, broken music stands torn and weathered music sheets and to few chairs to maintain sections. I have even seen students play while sitting on the radiator. The lock and chain that used to secure the equipment has been easily manipulated by students for years so when there is a sub or no teacher in the room they go in the "secured cage".

Down two ways to make education fun and easier for our students.

At the end of the hallway is an elevator. This elevator has been left in disrepair for years. It's use was for disabled students to go from floor to floor as well as for the AV squad to transport the equipment to classes on the second floor. Teachers have been left to find ways to get the equipment to any second floor classroom or not use visual aids in their presentation Later on you will hear about all the many laws being broken in cases of disability; Physical, Emotional and Learning.

Down four ways to make education easier for our children.

The science labs are ill-equipped for the courses being offered ie: Forensics and some of the classrooms have been known to have chemicals that have been in the same place for twenty or thirty years. Surely toxic if knocked over and broken maybe even explosive.

Down five ways to make education more viable for students.

Outside the student/athletes are forced to run on a track that has long been outdated Lately in the off-seasons grass grows in the cinder and the kids have to run a path into the track. The tracks have had to visit other schools for all meets because Roosevelt doesn't have a track. Doesn't have the four tennis courts needed for all home matches, Doesn't even have a legal sized basketball court and for the use that the football field endures something should be done. How about doing what all the other school are doing going with turf. but for right now proper water and fertilizer would help and the locker rooms . . . . It is really embarrassing that in this day and age there is no sports facility that would bring this town into the new millennium and also prevent over use of the high school fields especially since soccer has become so popular.

I could go on but the time I spent writing this could be a waste if we are just going to engage in rhetoric. Our children deserve the right to be much closer to a level playing field and we can't expect OBAMA to do it for us. Most of these problems are inherited by the Administration. But it is the alumni who could force the Board and higher to just give us back what we had. The colleges look for well rounded individuals when they read applications "Someone who will add to the college life of others"

One final note: during my years at Roosevelt many of my friends and classmates took Auto shop and other shop classes. Others took BOCES training for Cosmetology etc. A trade or the foundation for further application yielded more options. The ideology that Roosevelt kids should all be in academic only classes as well as refusing to pay for students to go to BOCES is naïve and a great injustice to the students and the drop out rate. Feel the power of this great membership and bring Change

Give the kids a reason to feel the same way you do about "the Velt".

O MY Roosevelt

Good Morning my Roosevelt; 7/27/06

As I leave my home south of Washington Avenue on my morning walk, I meditate. My route takes me down Decatur to Washington Avenue, across the bridge to Merrick, back across the bridge and through Roosevelt Park and on a good day to Clinton Ave before my return home. Having moved here in 1968, my meditation is often retrospective in nature. As I approach Washington Avenue there are three issues that come to mind.

Firstly, before the late "sixties" Washington Avenue was the "Mason-Dixon Line" that separated the races. Blacks to the South, Whites to the North. The second issue pops into my mind almost immediately when I think of the reasons why the Roosevelt Public Library has only one in-depth account of the history of Roosevelt which begins as far back as the 1600's and ends in 1960. Thirdly, I am deeply saddened to know that once this town went black that nobody cared enough to document the history of this town. For example, across from the library is the very first building of its kind acknowledging the very fine work that the PAL (Jim Simpson, George Jones, Charles Dudley etc.) has done to develop kids. But that building, nor their work has been documented and I think it is equally saddening that the history was completed by a man named Harry D. Daniels, who has a school in our district named after him but never mentioned an African-American in his historical account. There was mention of a small group of KKK members in town. From one other study we know that at least two black families lived on the south side back in the "thirties" and since the area around UB (formerly Theodore Roosevelt Elementary) was the "Negro" area it is no surprise to me why UB is falling apart and Centennial, it's sister school is the anchor for the school transition during construction.

Presently, Harry D. Daniels has more Afro-centric flavor then any other school in the district thanks to Ms. Charthern. I think we should be changing the name of the school to reflect our history. But now that the doors have been closed maybe we should wait and see what it is before we change names. Furthermore, UB should be called Julius Erving Elementary. I might need to interject here that the library is not at fault for this situation They are the keepers of the history not the recorders.

As I walk down Washington from Decatur extending to the bridge is the Cerebral Palsy Center. A spacious campus, beautifully manicured, immaculate buildings on both sides of the street and growing everyday. They do very fine work as well but being a child who grew up in town I realize that their facilities have always been better than those offered to the residents of this town. I did often wonder why the center was so neatly tucked away on the south side of Washington Avenue and then I remembered what the old negative mentality was about disabled individuals before the year of the Handicapped in 1987, I believe. Yes then they were cripples. One step above those living behind them.

At the foot of the Cerebral Palsy property is a bridge. This bridge crosses the Meadowbrook Parkway. Many Roosevelt residents do not know about this area and therefore do not use this bridge and the folks who travel across from the other side, many of them white, do not know about Roosevelt. They make that first turn in to the parking lot, they go back across the bridge to eat from the deli or Chinese and then they go back across at day's end.

I remember how during my college years, while home for a visit, a small group of white kids tried to lure me into an area on the other side of the fences by the parkway so that they could jump me. They acted as if they were beating some one else up and then yelled to me "aren't you going to help him" and I kept walking. They began to walk behind me and then I dropped one part of my Nun-chucks down from my sleeve and when I turned around they were making it back across the bridge.

As I walk back across the bridge back into Roosevelt I see five Town of Hempstead street sweepers crossing the bridge. What has been remarkable to me is for years these trucks have been stored at the end of Clinton Avenue and leave the plant on a daily basis, ignoring the leaves and trash in Roosevelt in order maintain and beautify other towns' spotless streets. My Roosevelt why do we allow these things to happen?

I enter Roosevelt Park through it's south gate and I look over a pretty lake that was once stocked by the County yearly so that people could fish. During the winters, I remember seeing the truck out on the ice testing weight capacity. If the ice was not safe there would be signs posted "No Skating Today". These pleasant thoughts are completely disrupted now by what I see as I pass by the Tennis and Basketball courts. Complete destruction. Who plans the renovation of a park in the middle of a summer? In a African-American neighborhood; One of the most vital resources for all the camps and daycares in town. Disruption of a Tennis program that has functioned for over thirty years as well as a youth summer basketball league. Some have told me that the problems of Roosevelt start at the schools. The elected officials are responsible for the Socio-economic issues and who do they come to when votes are needed; the religious officials. But we say we want to stop gangs!!!

Between this summer and the Contingency school budget set for September this will probably be the best recruit class yet for the gangs. What else is there to do? Mentoring? Mentoring is only good when you have programs connected to facilitate the youth's transition. The kids say "there is nothing to do" and that was before the last 90 days.

I know some of you have become old but you can counsel us younger folks from a chair. I know some of you are working too many jobs but you wouldn't have to bribe your kids to success if you spent a little community time. I hate to be redundant but it does take a whole village to raise a child. Can I wake you up tomorrow morning for a walk?

Sheldon Parrish

Good morning, 6/29/06

For those of you who well intended to be with me this morning and could not be, I prayed for you. I stood alone this morning but I have no problem with that because there will be another day that I will have to stand alone. But I do pray that you are blessed by association. My prayer went a little like this.

The Lord is my light and my salvation
Whom shall I fear
The Lord is the strength of my life
Of whom shall I be afraid.

Most Holy and Omnipotent Father I come this morning first to say I thank you for all you have done. For the blessings seen and unseen. Father I ask your blessing upon the Roosevelt School District. We need a "Valley experience" in this place. Father, I ask that you bless the buildings Father from door to door and from post to post. I ask Father that you bless the Superintendent as he makes the decisions that are most viable to the district.

Bless the Administrators. As they lead, let them exude their learned skills but show compassion for those they lead.

Bless the teachers Father as they negotiate for their livelihood, let them be covered with your Blood as they teach the children from their hearts. Let those who will be looking for a job find the blessing they deserve. Bless all the other staff members as they maintain a sound, safe and clean environment.

Bless the children for they are most affected by all actions. And Father even in their right to voice their opinion, give them guidance in the way they will go. I pray Father for our Personnel Director Father, who is standing in the need of prayer. I ask that you cover all with your blood during these turbulent times. And let the devil have no influence over your people.

These blessings I ask in the name of Jesus. Amen. Be Blessed

Oh Boy!!!!,

First Robert I feel we could take a mental tour around Roosevelt High School. If we start in the 100 wing to the right you will find kitchens Honeymooners set to teach Home Careers great place for me to volunteer and teach students how to make my Gumbo. Most of the classrooms to the right have windows that don't open and these classrooms have been used until the end of June. So glad we have a middle-school now.!! As a coach I have traveled to many school district's that have electronic bathrooms, you know the ones that would be so much more helpful when Mono breaks out. It gives us all the option of not touching things. Some years ago a radio/ TV station was built, A watt hasn't pass through as long as I have known of its existence.

Hey Rob remember the planetarium (State of the Art) Other school districts took field trips to Roosevelt just to have a Todd Schlegel production. Completely gutted now it serves as a Teacher's lounge, As you go further down that wing you see brand new lockers that have been there for years, not completely assembled. So the kids are starting to destroy them The same cage gate stands in the band room but if you leave it locked and go to the rest room all the kids are inside when you get back and some of the same French horns that when I left there as a student in 1976 still reside. They taste real brassy.

As you leave and turn the corner headed to the library you have an elevator that hasn't been functional since the last war. Students on the second floor often went without tech equipment because it could not be brought to them.

When I was a student the G.O. and other student organizations galvanized us to be a part of the process????????? (That is what your cable does when you choose a channel that is not operational) These org gave the student body more pride,

We must first show this sort of Galva nation to kids by not allowing people from all over the world come in and work on their doctorate, prove their thesis and then begonia. Worst ever Roosevelt—decision—Remove shop classes.

Rob there was even a principal who came in and took the Rough Rider off the floor and replaced with an R because that was how they did at W oh excuse me. Well there have been a lot of student athletes who have sweat, lead and cried for that Rough Rider. How dare her!!! Needless to say it returned after her departure. As a town and as a school district we need to take our stuff back. There are no young Emily Moore's (Check the history . . . .). If I go any farther Rob my book would be redundant

Integration Dream Lost in Roosevelt

By Joye Brown Staff Writer

Once upon a time, there was a place in virtually all-white Long Island that civil rights activists pointed to as integrated. That place was Roosevelt, one square mile of homes and businesses.

Mrs. Michael Zaffe favored racial balance (Newsday Photo/Dick Kraus)

At that time, the community of 14,000 was also about 30 percent black. Yet, "there has been little, if any, racial tension and bitterness," noted a 1965 newspaper story.

The community boasted a movie theater, bowling alley and skating rink. It was not uncommon for residents to leave their doors unlocked as they walked to plentiful shopping nearby. But cracks already were beginning to show. That same year, the newspaper reported, black civic activists "launched a fight to keep a stabilized neighborhood of single-family homes, a community that ranks in the middle-income group or higher, a place that would be free of blighted areas."

But in the next few years, as the community increasingly became a place where blacks wanted to live, it became a place whites rushed to leave. And they took with them many businesses, services and the guarantee of schools that graduated mostly college-bound students. Like many communities, such as Lakeview and Uniondale, Roosevelt's years of blacks and whites sharing equally in suburban life were fleeting. "Study after study shows that white people have little tolerance for racial minorities living nearby, especially African-Americans," said Marc Silver, a sociologist at Hofstra University. "Unfortunately, with white flight comes an association with declining property values, higher taxes, absentee landlords and decreasing community services." In the late '60s, when fights over integrating Roosevelt schools landed in court, white flight accelerated. Real estate speculators moved in. And properties owned by absentee landlords opened up a lucrative rental market. By 1970, the transformation was complete; Roosevelt became almost all black. Now, it has a sizable black middle-class population. But

Community life is not what it was. "One problem is that single-family homeowners were not replaced with single-family homeowners," said Robert Francis, commissioner of planning and economic development for the Town of Hempstead and a Roosevelt resident for 33 years. "Over time, there were more people per home, which caused overcrowding and strained services, especially in the schools. The problem became not so much race as economics."

In that, Roosevelt could be a lesson on what went wrong in the maturing of suburbia. In his study of the 22 counties surrounding New York City in 1957, Harvard sociologist Oscar Hadlin accurately predicted that more and more blacks would seek their place in the suburbs. He predicted that blacks probably would settle together—just as other immigrants had. But, he warned that without acceptance from whites, blacks would not share the amenities suburbia had to offer. "When color and ethnic identity cease to be unbearable burdens, when opportunity for jobs, education and housing becomes genuinely equal . . . the Negroes . . . will at least have a firm base upon which to construct a sound communal life . . . The alternative in a democratic society is almost unthinkable," Hadlin wrote.

In Roosevelt, civic leaders today contend with the unthinkable, continuing efforts to bring Roosevelt back to the community it was three decades ago. "I see single-family homes being built," said Francis, "and that's a good sign. But are we where we were back in the 1960s? I don't think so." *Copyright © 2007, Newsdav* Roosevelt, New York—Wikipedia, the free encyclopedia
http://en.wikipedia.org/wiki/Roosevelt, NewYork

Roosevelt, New York

Roosevelt is a hamlet (and census-designated place) in Nassau County, New York, United States. The population was 15,854 at the 2000 census. Roosevelt is in the Town of Hempstead.

Roosevelt is one of the few African-American majority CDPs on Long Island. Known colloquially as Da Velt, it has the reputation of having more poverty and less school funding than other Long Island areas.

Contents

Education

Roosevelt is considered the worst school district in New York State and was taken over by the state Education Department in 2002 after several years of warnings and failed reform efforts. Despite the new administration and constant state monitoring, Roosevelt's students have continued to perform well below established state standards. Last year, by eighth grade, only 10% of Roosevelt's students passed the math assessment and only slightly more passed the English Language Arts test (2006 statistics). Roosevelt High School has serious trouble with its students graduating despite the district's relatively large budget of $63 million.

Thanked God Dr. Tucker and Ms. Solomon have changed those numbers.

Geography

Roosevelt is located at 40°40'45"N, 73°35'8"W (40.679172,—73.585471) GR1

According to the United States Census Bureau, the CDP has a total area of 4.6 km² (1.8 miz). 4.6 kmz (1.8 Mil) of it is land and 0.56% is water.

Demographics (2007)

As of the census[GR2] of 2000, there were 15,854 people, 4,061 households, and 3,362 families residing in the CDP. The population density was 3,438.9/km^2 (8,916.8/miz). There were 4,234 housing units at an average density of 918.4/km^2 (2,381.3/miz). The racial makeup of the CDP was 7.97% White, 79.02% African American, 0.46%

Native American, 0.49% Asian, 0.05% Pacific Islander, 8.33% from other races, and 3.69% from two or more races. Hispanic or Latino of any race were 16.22% of the population.

There were 4,061 households out of which 38.3% had children under the age of 18 living with them, 44.2% were married couples living together, 30.3% had a female householder with no husband present, and 17.2% were

Trivia

Do you remember?

The Hoagie House
Cleanerama
A&P across the street
Benny Rhodes
Roosevelt Movie
Steer Inn
Club Chateau
Mr.Hicks Place
Corner Inn
Blessing Center
Kentucky Fried Chicken
Sweet Clover Dairy
Colony Furniture
Holmes Liquors
Diner(Mansfield Ave)

Nassau Rd. 2 lanes
Old A&P(Charles Cleaners building)
CEDShop
Club Shaft
Sportsman 30
Roller Rink
Chateau Lounge
Ice Cream Parlor(next to bank)
HYWAY Inn
Douglas Funeral Home
Dairy Barn
Beverage House (Freeport borderline)
Pre-K Nassau Rd.
Camera Shop
Buster Brown Shoes Store

In Conclusion

I T IS HARD to believe that a trip to the Roosevelt Public Library brought this project to fruition. It is equally hard to believe that almost 3 years later the fire still burns vehemently yearning to be extinguished. The catalyst behind the fire, an author by the name of Harry D. Daniels. His story ended in 1960 and although African-Americans existed there was little mentioned but more about Klan Activity. I hope at some point someone leads a petition effort to change the name of that school.

My senior year we were on austerity and in order to play sports businessmen in town partnered with Dr. J. and the Nets in order to raise the funds. There was a big media event in Penn Station in Manhattan in which Corliss Bailey and I represented the student body and Converse did a billboard promotion. There was a poster created using Roosevelt students that was posted in train stations around the city. I remember cheerleader Wendy Abraham being in that poster as well.

Recently, after a great career and a tenure as an ambassador to the NBA, Dr. J. was named to the Basketball Hall of Fame as well as being named one of the "Fifty Best" players in NBA history. I also believe it would be a great gesture for Roosevelt to name Centennial Ave school after Mr. Charles McIlwain former principal, representing his almost half century of service as well as being the first African-American educator in Roosevelt. I would not hesitate to extend myself to the point of stating that Emily Moore should even be considered due to her length of service to the school district as well as the community. Unmatchable in her approach, sometimes controversial we have all benefited from "The Struggle." I think some of us have forgotten that it is the controversy that affects change. Those who stand up front are always called the troublemakers, but in this society "the squeaky wheel gets the oil". We may never have had a staff that looked more like us or African-American curriculum subjects had it not been for the struggled. The results may not be so evident today as in the last ten years or more people from outside the community have come in and sabotaged that effort. What mindset is our present personnel director engaged in?

I can remember a time when African-American male educators were plentiful at Roosevelt High School. Alumni have often mentioned their gratitude an thanks to the mentorship of teachers like Mr. Brandon, Mr. R. Brown, Mr. J Bryant, Mr. Harvey Palmore, Mr. L. Franklin, Mr. Donnell Nash, Mr. B. Rapelyea, Mr. K. Brown etc. and now only Mr. D. Crummell and Mr. K. Johnson stand in the gap with more than 10 years of experience. Somebody should do a study to find out how many of these African-Americans males have been able to retire from the school district as opposed to non-African-Americans in what has mainly been an African-American town and community.

Roosevelt I have loved you from the very start, Yeah and as I flashback I remember how I was treated when I first came to town. I moved from the Pomonoc Apartment complex in Queens where I mostly went to school with Jewish kids. I did not know the ways of Brooklyn, Harlem and the Bronx. I didn't have real friends and so you slapped me and jumped me but when I became the person I needed to become in order to deal with you I took no revenge and chalked it up to becoming that "Manchild" called Crusher. Alumni Stevie Bell and Billy Scott gave me that name in the locker room before practice one day and it stuck.

The start of my transition began with pledging the "Gold and Blue". Then my lunch money stayed in my pocket and the only other obstacle as a Junior Varsity football player was avoiding the trap Varsity ballplayers had waiting for us when we took our equipment downstairs to dry after practice everyday. There was "a cage" and when they saw enough of us young boys in the cage they would cut the lights out and start swinging. We had to protest taking our stuff downstairs. It was then that I dispelled another rumor; NO POOL. But the rifle range was down there. I miss the days of pep rallies that had the whole building excited not looking for a way to sneak home early.

I miss seeing the custodial staff dumping donated wood products on the softball field leading up to homecoming weekend. I miss Friday night leading my teammates out for the Bon Fire/Pep Rally and then getting out of the Homecoming Dance before Coach came looking for us. I like to dance so I remember doing the "Skate" to Potential by the Jimmy Castor Bunch and having a circle around me and my dance partner. Me and Tracy Randleman went at it one night while Hank and Keith, The Spectrum Crew were doing the music, of course. Charlie Mahoney, fellow co-captain tapped me on the shoulder to tell me one our teammates had overdone his celebration and we needed to take him home and I was the only one driving that night. I will never know how he played the next day because cheap wine was fashionable then. We even sang our victory song about wine. If we were on the bus we would take turns with our lines as the rest of the team would say in unison (Oh Yeah!) "Its in my eye (Oh Yeah) that Bali High, "It's the word (Oh Yeah!) That Thunderbird. I guess they stopped singing the song years later after everybody wanted to sing about the "Chunky Black" and most of the wines don't exist anymore.

The places used for dances outside of the school were "The Queen" of Most Holy Rosary gym and the VFW hall on Brookside which is now Tabernacle of Joy. But things were peaceful then and it wasn't about "wildin' or later bangin".

I'd had forgotten another institution called the Senior Show. My first senior show was as a ninth grader class of '73. I remember Jimmy Douglas and James Simpson Jr. (Junebug) and two other guys were the Emcees for the night. They walked down the four aisles of the auditorium to four different Love Ballads. That was when I first heard Million Dollars by Soul Generation, a personal all-time favorite.

The following year I had joined a band with some of the most talented young boys. I say young boys because some of the guys had older brothers who were know as musicians. The band was Black Exodus; Michael Spencer, Michael Sanders, Howard Wyche, Wayne Speller, Phillip McDowell, Tony Williams, Russell Edwards, Michael and John Wortham and myself. We auditioned for the Class of 74 senior Show with four other bands. We were the first selected of three. There was some controversy because I believe two of the bands not chosen were members of that class and we were sophomores at the time. They were also good bands but we had a tight horn section and a "Kool and the Gang" medley; Funky Stuff, Hollywood Swinging, Jungle Boogie that rocked em'. It was a shame that we headed in different directions because that was a good band.

For someone who started out "shaky", I graduated with accolades "Most Athletic", "Most Masculine" and one of the top 44 football players in Nassau County '75-'76, but most of all bleeding Gold and Blue. I started the Parrish tradition in 1973 and my son concluded his senior season in 2008 and my nephew will graduate in 2009. My son duplicated my football awards and I thank the community for all their help because it still takes "a whole community to raise a child". As players and then as coaches on behalf of the Parrish's, Todd, Terence and I would like to thank the community of Roosevelt for the opportunity to represent you as well as mentor thousands of your kids. To all that was Gold and Blue, with such Pride and Dignity, I say Cudos, Job Well Done. To all those who sweat and toiled to make the town a strong and vibrant town I salute you and with this project you will be forever recorded in history of Roosevelt's," One Square Mile"

Photo Memories

Dr. Earl Franklin Mosely

SHELDON PARRISH

ANDY KERR STADIUM

1976 COLGATE UNIVERSITY FOOTBALL TEAM

Section 8 Football Individual Playoff Game Records

Touchdowns: 7 — Rob Smith, Wantagh vs. Floral Park, November 12, 2004

Yards Gained Rushing: 397 — Bryant Daniels, South Side vs. Lawrence, November 23, 2001 (34 carries)

Yards Gained Passing: 273 — Chris Kupek, Syosset vs. Garden City, November 14, 1970 (14-19) (14 for 19)

Touchdown Passes: 4 — Jim Aberasturi, Hewlett vs. Lawrence, November 17, 1996 (4 OT)

Brian Rath, Wantagh vs. Plainedge, November 16, 2001

Randy Mills, Freeport vs. Hempstead, November 15, 2003

Steve Probst, Farmingdale vs. Uniondale, November 3, 2006

Completions: 24 — Kevin Lowe, Mineola vs. Bethpage, November 24, 1989 (24 for 38)

Receptions: 12 — Aaron Valentin, Freeport vs. Massapequa, November 11, 2004

Touchdown Receptions: 4 — Joe Holden, Wantagh vs. Plainedge, November 16, 2001

Yards Receiving: 176 — Bill Carey, South Side vs. MacArthur, November 15, 2001

Joe Holden, Wantagh vs. Plainedge, November 16, 2001

Field Goals: 2 — Tom Boccafola, Farmingdale vs. Long Beach, November 22, 1986

Peter Kaufman, Hewlett vs. Lawrence, November 17, 1996

Steve Thompson, Wantagh vs. Floral Park, November 15, 1998

Longest Field Goal. 49 yds. — Jon Marigliano, Locust Valley vs. Oyster Bay, November 19, 1987

Extra Points: 8 — Trevor Michaelsen, Bethpage vs. West Hempstead, November 16, 2002

Longest Punt: 83 yds. — Brian Pagano, Plainedge vs. Bethpage, November 17, 1990

Interceptions: 3 — Chamari Willis, Lawrence vs. Hewlett, November 17, 1996

Jim Cerullo, Massapequa vs. Freeport, November 22, 1997

Jamaal Salah, Roosevelt vs. Manhasset, November 22, 1997

Quincy Hankins, Roosevelt vs. Seaford, November 18, 2006

Fumble Recoveries: 4 — Chris Caine, MacArthur vs. Hewlett, November 16, 2002

Longest Touchdown Plays:

Rushing — 99 yds. — Jim Teaton, Farmingdale vs. Westbury, November 20, 1971

Passing — 86 yds. — Frank Baglivo to Ronnie Modik, Island Trees vs. Bethpage, November 4, 2006

Kick-off Return — 97 yds. — Josh Huggins, Freeport vs. Syosset, November 11, 2000

Craig Alek-Finkelman, Clarke vs. Roosevelt, November 21, 2003

Punt Return — 83 yds. — Max Seibald, Hewlett vs. Calhoun, November 6, 2004

Interception — 98 yds. — Alex Mauro, Locust Valley vs. North Shore, November 4, 2006

Fumble Return — 98 yds. — William Mingo, Roosevelt vs. Malverne, November 18, 1989

20 YARD LINE OVERTIME TIE-BREAKING PROCEDURE

1. If at the end of the fourth quarter, the teams have identical scores, the tie may be resolved by this plan. All game rules will apply except the try is not required to break the tie.

2. When the score is tied at the end of the fourth quarter, the referee will instruct both teams to return to their respective team boxes. There will be a three minute intermission during which both teams may confer with their coaches. All officials will assemble at the 50 yard line, review the procedure and determine the number of time-outs remaining for each team. The head linesman will go to the team on the side of the field where the line-to-gain equipment is located. The field judge will go to the other to inform the coaches of the number of time-outs each team has remaining and escort the respective team captains to the center of the field for the coin toss. The visiting team captain shall be given the privilege of calling the coin while it is in the air. The winner of the toss shall be given his choice of the ball possession or designating the direction of the offense for the overtime period.

3. Each team shall be permitted one additional time-out for each extra period plus any unused regulation game time-out. The team scoring the greater number of points in the overtime shall be declared the winner. The final score shall be determined by totaling all points scored by each team during the regulation and overtime periods.

4. To start the overtime, the offensive team shall put the ball in play, first and 10 on B's 20 yard line. Team A shall have a series of four downs to make a first down (10 yards). The series shall be terminated by any score by A or if B has possession at the end of any down. Team A shall be awarded a new series when: (a) the penalty for defensive pass interference is accepted; (b) there is a change of team possession during the down and the ball belongs to A at the end of the down; (c) team A recovers a scrimmage kick (field goal attempt) between the goal lines after it has been touched first by B beyond the neutral zone; (d) when any penalty by B results in a next series being awarded; (e) when the line to gain is made.

5. If team A scores a touchdown, it is entitled to the opportunity to try for the point, except when it is unnecessary to break the tie. A field goal attempt is permitted on any down.

6. After team A has completed its series, team B will become the offensive team with the ball in its possession at the 20 yard line. The same end of the field will be used for both possessions in order to insure equal game conditions and conserve time.

7. If the score remains tied after each team has been given one series, the procedure shall be repeated until a winner is determined. There will be an intermission of two minutes, during which the loser of the toss will be given first choice of options. If additional periods are required, first choice of options will be alternated.

Roosevelt Wins

—Continued from Back Page

drove the left baseline for a layup, Bryant hit a 15-footer from the left wing and Brown made two free throws with 2:04 remaining, giving Roosevelt a 49-46 edge. Woodlands managed to tie the score at 50 on Mark Shumley's eight-foot turnaround shot, but two foul shots by Melvin Fichett with 34 seconds left and two more by Brown with 17 seconds to go put Roosevelt in front, 54-50. Shumley converted an offensive rebound with nine seconds to go, but two free throws by Brown with six seconds left sealed the victory for Roosevelt.

"I wasn't nervous at all," said Brown, who made seven of eight free throws in the final two minutes. "What was there to be nervous about? Every time I went to the line I said to myself, it's just a foul shot, that's all it is.'"

Roosevelt proves a winner when game is on the line

Roosevelt Wins

2 Suffolk Swimmers Win St...

Island Sweeps Regionals

Wyandanch Pl... Wins Class C Ta...

Rough Riders Win Class B Championship

Roosevelt Gets Its 1st No-Hitter With Harris' 11-Strikeout Gem

SHELDON PARRISH

Gridiron 2008

Congratulations Gridiron Team
Especially
Roosevelt Rough Riders

All County
3 - Jalon Edwards
7 - Korye Hollingsworth
54 - Sir Parrish
68 - Scott Wright

All-Conference
4 - Jawara Dudley
8 - James McClenic

Thorn Award
Robert Lee — 1985
Jerone Pettus — 1999

Martens Award
Elliott Fortune — 1991
Randall James — 2000

1999, 2004
Rutgers Cup

1999, 2000, 2004, 2006
Long Island Champions

Rough Riders
1 Wagner Avenue, Roosevelt, NY 11575
(516) 345-7216

Sierra White

BOMB SQUAD : VERSION 2.2 : DESTRUCTION

Sisters

In

The

Struggle!

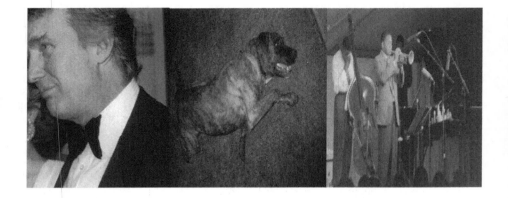

The Sister Minister Seretta C. McKnight
President

22 July 2007

FALL FANTASY

Prologue	Nathaniel Bailey
Welcome	Mr. J. Watkins
Devotion	EMMK
Solace	Kendrick Reid
Accompanied By	Philip Hall
Proclamation of Coronation	William Vaughn
Processional	Autumn Leaves
Introduction of the Court	Ms. Williams
	Miss Sword
Coronation	Mr. P. Smith
Crown Bearer	Todd Parrish
Queen's Response	Michelle Butler
Serenade to the Queen	EMMK
"Three Times a Lady"	
Dream Variations	Frances Mackey
Sweetheart Presentation	Mr. Wallace
	Terence Parrish
Sweetheart's Response	Raquel Mason
Sweetheart Serenade	Carolyn Harding
"If You Believe"	
Recessional	Philip Hall
Epilogue	Sylvia McLendon
Musical Selection	EMMK

HIGH SCHOOLS

Roosevelt Gets Its 1st No-Hi With Harris' 11-Strikeout G

ONE SQUARE MILE

177

SHELDON PARRISH

All pictures present were either part of the Parrish collections or obtained from the Roosevelt Alumni Association Website.

Made in the USA
Lexington, KY
12 April 2017